D1442827

CONSTRAINED
ATTITUDES

CONSTRAINED ATTITUDES

By

FRANK MOORE COLBY

Essay Index Reprint Series

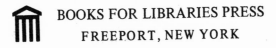

BOOKS FOR LIBRARIES PRESS
FREEPORT, NEW YORK

First Published 1910
Reprinted 1968

LIBRARY OF CONGRESS CATALOG CARD NUMBER:

68-8449

PRINTED IN THE UNITED STATES OF AMERICA

CONTENTS

CORAM POPULO

I

CORAM POPULO

SOUND and able men, no doubt, and men whom the nation delights to honour, but what does happen to you as you grasp the pen or mount the platform? For many years have I pondered this strange public diminution of the private man, bursting out on the subject now and then in print, and to this day I cannot read a newspaper, attend an alumni dinner, incline my mind to thoughts presidential or leading citizens' ideals, without a sense of wonder. And though sheer bald wonder may seem to some to be of small advantage, I do assure all who, like me, are sometimes a little wearied on these occasions that it helps to pass the time.

CONSTRAINED ATTITUDES

Newspapers are no less merciless to their writers than they are to their readers. It is a cruel thing, this system which effaces completely the editorial person, good or bad, and leaves only a vague " we," meaning the corporation, or the linotype machines, or the people, or some such bundle of entities, never anybody in particular. A sad personal disaster behind that corporate " we." Sometimes there is the wail of a lost soul in it—somebody trying to be everybody and all gone to vulgar fractions in the process. There are editors who think exclusively in " we's," even out of office hours, the mind balking instinctively at any thought " unlikely to interest our readers " or unsupported by an " influential portion of the intelligent public." That is what comes of being a mouthpiece and a fourth estate, and a bulwark, palladium, wholesale broker in public opinion, guide, caterer, social

4

dynamometer and what not. An editor's soul will usually disappear long before it leaves the body.

Editorial expression at present is so impersonal that nobody seems to matter in the least. A massacre in Park Row, provided it did not end in pillage, would make little difference in those excellent editorial pages. Should the murderers pass from Franklin Square (wet with the blood of Harper's chivalry) to the offices of uptown monthly magazines, pausing only to burn the editors of the two admirable weeklies which they would pass on the way, the carnage, though in a sense deplorable, would not seriously affect the characters of the bereaved magazines. A momentary maladjustment, perhaps, some black-bordered paragraphs about an irreparable loss, but soon each would be giving to its readers precisely what its readers were accustomed to receive. And but for those same black borders no reader would suspect that the " strong personality which left its impress on all its pages " had recently " passed away." I would not bring back the times when editors were shot or horse-whipped for what they wrote, yet I do miss the kind of man whose absence would be noticed if by chance somebody did kill him.

Others have expressed the same feeling of loneliness while wandering among the printed words of college presidents. I remember, however, that one college president did speak out on a public occasion about eleven years ago, and it caused no small excitement. He advised, I think, the social ostracism of wicked millionaires. The thought itself was not remarkable. It was familiar indeed from several Bible texts. But it did seem a valiant thought for a college president. The standard of college presidents is not that of other men; it is more nearly that set by Pericles for women. It is not desired that they shall stir the public thought or divide the minds of citizens. The moral and intellectual caution demanded of them in the public gaze has always been enormous. A humanly applicable remark is a presidential indecency. In contrast to the wild turbulence of the home, where Christian sentiments may be rudely noised and the Ten Commandments flung about without regard to whom they injure, the American citizen has ever turned to the college presidential platform as to the centre of repose. No tampering with conscience from that quarter at all events; no personal application; no shock from collision with a mind in motion. Hence it was most natural when this college president applied a principle of the Bible to human affairs that a thousand editorial writers should begin writing passionately at once and that many of us should exclaim, The daredevil! Privately he would have seemed quite tame and dull; presidentially he was a madcap.

Never but once have I been stirred on an important college occasion. This was at a Commencement dinner, where, carried away by my feelings, I almost made a speech. This was the speech I came near making:

"It is not often, Mr. President, brother alumni, and distinguished guests, that I rise to appreciable heights of moral grandeur, but I do so now. I stand before you to-night, brimming with the spirit of your recent addresses. I, too, have my generalities and my truisms, and it will do you no harm to listen in your turn to my somewhat nasal moral singsong. Through a chain of flowery Junes, reaching far beyond the memory of men now living, may be traced both the form and the substance of your speeches. For no law of nature

8

CONSTRAINED ATTITUDES

seems more sure than this great law of Commencement gravitation, whereby it is ruled that the heavy bodies of like "distinguished sons" shall fall in like manner upon their subjects. Such is the force of tradition, and this is the traditon of June, that for many days the minds of our youth shall be soused in the cant of their elders and a land already drugged with optimism shall again be overdosed. But a time-honoured tradition, gentlemen, is not necessarily a good tradition, as we know from that most ancient and best beloved of human institutions, the lie. Here let us pause to consider the peril concealed in what may be called American college platform English, that is to say, the large, loose, general and roseate language you have just now employed. It is ambiguous; there is room in it, alas! for wicked things. Your alma mater has grown richer; so has the lie. She has a larger entering class than in

9

any past year of her history; so has the lie. She has added several new courses, each with an endowed professorship; so has that older but no less progressive institution, the lie— that incomparable alma mater by your own tests of alma-maternity, for are not her alumni the most numerous, the most glorious and the most loyal of them all? For the tests are still only success and numbers. Still that doxology of success and numbers. Still after fifty Junes the young man "going forth into the world" may learn from his oratorical elders only the piety of success and the wisdom of numbers. The "plain people" still perceive that your Commencement exhortation will, after drawing off the water, yield only that. I rise for one moment on the backbone of this republic to inquire, Is this well?"

These ringing words were not spoken and perhaps it is as well that they were not, for the

10

mysteries of college eloquence are not for me to solve.

But the charms wrought by educators on other educators and on those whom they have educated are after all not nearly so strange as the magic words of Chief Executives. What spells were once cast, for example, by Presidential language such as this: " Purity in politics is laudable, and if we would be good citizens we must insist on good laws, and what this country needs is manly men (equally, of course, womanly women, for woman is very important; so is the home), and if we are poor, let us not envy the rich, and if we are rich let us not despise the poor, for a man's a man for a' that, and our lives should be both strenuous and simple, and let us take for our constant example the youth who bore through snow and ice the banner with the strange device, U-pi-dee, i-da." Where are these wildfolk, clad in

11

goatskins, and possibly anthropophagous in taste, whom the mere remark that it is better to be good than bad so strangely moves? I have never met a single person who owned to any special liking for the thing, although my acquaintance includes some of the simplest types of human life as yet known to science. No matter how plain and honest our fellow-citizen may be, he always appears somewhat blasé, and passes it on to some one else whom he believes to be still plainer.

It was expected of Presidents, ex-Presidents and the like that they would rise in public at short intervals and plead for the home. It seemed probable that every future President would find that a fixed part of his duties as chief magistrate was the almost incessant championship of motherhood. Official praises of the home accompanied by bugle calls to domesticity were felt to be the country's daily need. That is why one ex-President (himself a superb family man and every inch a husband) paused so seldom in his advocacy of the home. That is why another ex-President, by no means an emotional person, once came forward to defend the home, braving the slings of cankered club-women. Soon or late every leading citizen addressed himself in public (à propos of nothing in particular) to the absorbing questions, How is Woman and How is the Home? Domestic as we were already—doing our very best, one might fairly say—we were stampeded every other day ·by vague but excited exhortation to rally round the home. Hearing for the thousandth time that they ought to stay at home and rear good citizens, a number of American club-women retorted somewhat tartly to this advice. There is, I have noticed, a certain acerbity in the writings of club-women, implying that the Cause, though in the main benevolent, has its forbidding side. One of them, re-ferring to the idle habits of Presidents, de-clared that she "had heard of families that starved because the fathers went fishing all the time." Another said, "It is the plea of a man who speaks from a purely selfish standpoint, as though he were afraid his wife might become a club-woman." A third gave warning that the sight "of the President of the United States galloping over the country urging women to bear more children" would "engender the spirit of rebellion in the minds of many women."

While I do not sympathise with the vindic-tive spirit of these rejoinders, I believe that the anxieties of editors and statesmen on this sub-ject are excessive; that the most domestic peo-ple under the sun are entitled to their moments of self-confidence; that for days at a time Wo-man is safe and the home unshaken; that even in the absence of explicit advice, children would be born and raised, and that meals are cooked even in the pauses of oratory. And in not flying into print to the defence of the home, let me not for one moment be suspected of laxity. By Heaven! I should as soon think of hauling down Old Glory as of removing from above my fireplace that cardboard motto, "God Bless Our Home," stitched in worsted. I am opposed to cannibalism, polygamy, human sacrifice, the areois, polyandry, the suttee, the exposure of infants on Mount Taygetus, anarchy and feudalism. Civilisation has my endorsement, and the family tie in its hour of need may count on me for a word of encouragement. Silence on these themes now is no sign of heresy, but proof, rather, of a deep conviction that certain things may be taken for granted even among the people at large. The very plainest of the plain people are not without a certain sense of proportion, nor do they lack for

truisms in their daily life. They know that
the kitchen will subsist though undefended by
a leading citizen, and that the nursery is in a
fair way to hold its own. They know that if
the home has its renegades it has also its vic-
tims, and they can reckon up more mere wives
and utter husbands than they can count va-
grants from the marriage bond. They have
seen the family so absolutely a unit that each
member was socially an abject fraction, and
many a homelike city in this country has furnished a case in point; and if men have fallen
from fatherhood, they can point to many a
putative citizen who is too much of a father
for his country's good, and to pairs linked together in monosyllabic intimacy who were, if
anything, too much encouraged by this constant Presidential and editorial singing of
Home, Sweet Home. And so considering the
number and the kind of influences that home

16

ties do resist, they openly defy the most leonine of club-women to do her worst.

And lest it appear that I have nothing to complain of but a surfeit from these Presidential champions of the home, let me add a political argument, which I have drawn from a recent book on English manners. It is written by an American power-worshipper, whose admiration of the British widens with the square miles of their empire on the map. England, he says, has of late years been ruled by a "succession of mighty men," and if put to it he would no doubt explain that they were mighty because they ruled England. And this brings him to an aspect of England to which he frequently recurs, as well he may, for it is indeed charming. It is the aspect of England as the happy hunting-ground of husbands, the land where on moderate incomes the men have valets and the women hardly any

17

clothes. For the great capacity to rule, to conquer and to colonise may, he thinks, be traced directly to the male ascendancy in the English home. Groomed, well-fed, exercised, never thwarted, and with the wife always in her proper place, the English husband is, like the fire engine horse, always in the pink of condition, and ready at an instant's moral alarm to rush forth to the most distant part of the world and kill a coloured man. This explains the British empire, and, *per contra*, I may add, it explains the imperial shortcomings of the United States, for here having once provided for the wife in that station of life to which it has pleased her to call him, and having served without offence as handy man about the house, the American husband has not the time left, still less the spirit, to be off shooting Matabeles. Thus the question of empire is fought out in the home, and you often meet a husband, now utterly domesticated, whose abilities might, if his wife would only set them loose, make him a colonial governor. We have the manhood, could it but be disengaged.

However, these larger cares are not for me but only for opinion-moulders, world-workers, world-pushers, and their kind. Some say the nation profits from their language, even though no single person does, which is one of the mysteries of political arithmetic. Others complain that, like swearing, it takes the meaning out of words, or inflates the moral currency, or adds a touch of impotence to old familiar truths. Nothing, they say, makes concrete sinners feel so safe and sleepy as the distant rumble of the Golden Rule. The foreigner in his crude way calls it hypocrisy. To what extent it has helped to fill the jails or the high places in this country may some day be determined by a patient sociologist. But to the echo-beaten mind of a casual reader it is interesting rather as one of the numerous democratic liturgies, pen-habits, thought-saving devices or mental petrifactions which make so many public Americans seem allegorical. After all, except in public, there are really no such men.

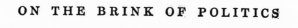

ON THE BRINK OF POLITICS

II

ON THE BRINK OF POLITICS

SOME time ago I read a book of an evolutionary cast on the irrationality of politics, in
which the writer devoted much time and en-
ergy to proving that political opinions were
formed generally in the dim twilight of the
human mind.

He complained that the student of politics
spent his time in analysing human institutions
and neglected the analysis of man. He said we
ought to know at least as much about man as
may be learned from a modern text-book on
psychology. He himself had entered politics
by way of biology and psychology, passing
thence directly into laboratory work as a Member of the British Parliament. With admirable

evolutionary modesty he repressed any political opinions of his own, noting merely the effect of party cries and iterated doctrines on other members of his species. He delighted in the relative view of things. He liked to trace a political emotion back through the savages to some fossil horse.

He usually stopped with these statements of kinship, leaving it to us to make the application. Occasionally, however, he did offer a practical suggestion. There was, for example, the common bond between cats and business men, between property-owners and squirrels, magpies and dogs. He desired some economist to write a treatise on the question, Would the property instinct "die away if not indulged"?

But as a rule he did not go beyond the proof of ancestry, for he was one of those tantalising social evolutionary persons whose thoughts end so completely in zoological circles that you cannot tell whether they write for the enlightenment of men or by way of courtesy to the lower animals. When he saw a politician, he immediately became absorbed in calculating the degree of moral credit due to angle-worms.

The danger of this social-evolutionary habit is that one's whole life may slip away in the making of zoological comparisons, allowing no time for reflecting on what they mean. Brought up as we have been in the evolutional tradition we are too apt already to be engrossed with unfruitful family resemblances, as between housewives and hens, caddis-worms and novelists, dogs and savings-bank depositors. I myself might easily write a chapter on the Functions of Polite Human Conversation That Were Once Performed by Tails. I should show how men were obliged to say Good-morning, because they found they had nothing left to wag it with, and how a great many social feelings once expressed without noise but with perfect accuracy by the tail were later driven to an oral outlet. Spoken greetings were not needed so long as there were tails. A tail declared that you were glad you could come; tails replied that your hosts were glad to see you. The time of day in that early period was always and effectively passed with the tail. Tails extended the early courtesies, hospitalities and good cheer, waved doubtful assent or cordial approval, differentiated the welcome of a friend from that of a bare acquaintance, sufficed in short for all the simple social amenities now expressed in forms of speech.

I should dissent from the scholarly Unsoweiter's well-known view that the need of articulate social sounds for the expression of the hitherto-tail-uttered emotions accelerated the development of primitive speech-forms. I should hold rather with the learned Zumbeispiel's more recent studies in "Tail Rhythms and Animal Benignity" that by thrusting upon the limited potentialities of primitive tongues the once-adequately-tail-performed social duties, the loss of the tail may well have retarded the development of more variegated idioms. I should agree with him that even in the highest known forms of modern society speech is burdened with social sentiments which are not only perfectly tail-utterable but could, indeed, be better and less laboriously rendered on that simpler and more responsive instrument. I should point to the misconstruction of social silence, the fear of the pause, the social dependence on audible signs of animation, and the unjust application of the stigma "grumpy" to really friendly persons who lack, for the moment, speech, but who with tails would, no doubt, involuntarily express the warmest social feelings.

27

And I should applaud heartily Zumbeispiel's conclusion that it is far too soon, perhaps by one and one-quarter million years, for civilised man to regard the loss of his earlier and more automatic social indicator with any other feeling than regret. In an appendix I should reproduce in a notation of measured tail-beats (based on duration and intensity of vibration) many entire conversations overheard at my club. I could, as I say, easily write such a chapter. I lack only a knowledge of biology to make myself well-nigh intolerable. But I shall never write it for a reason that seldom deters any modern social evolutionist—the reason that it seems a rather silly thing to do. Besides, I have little doubt that it has been already written.

But to return to the irrationality of politics. My writer seemed to think that he was alone in regarding politics as irrational. Again and again he would attack the " assumption so closely interwoven with our habits of political and economic thought that men always act on a reasoned opinion as to their interests." This seemed to me an assumption that fell down almost as soon as it was stated.

We do not in our private capacities assume that " men always act on a reasoned opinion as to their interests " when they vote any more than when they marry or when they dance. Mad as the world is we are spared that final, mind-closing illusion that it is sane. Surely there is a deep enough faith in the irrationality of our current politics. Even though we shrink from the horrid disclosures of self-examination there is always a friend to examine Who has not gazed giddily at the irrationality of a friend's politics? But the argument was perhaps addressed not to men in their private capacities, but to that far lower order of beings, men about to appear in public, men on the point of mounting platforms, getting ready to write leading articles, planning treatises on social science. For that portion of a man which is ready for publication or may be found at any time in a political speech such language may have a special use—if only as a reminder that there is more of him.

I doubt if there is any such widespread illusion in private life as to the rationality of politics. Publicly we express leadership in terms of the leader's ability; privately we think it in terms of the dulness of the led. No one needs proof that men rise in politics not because they are weighty but because they are light; and the forlorn human tatters to be seen at any time floating even in light political breezes are the subject of common remark. When the strong wind of free silver bore upward the expanding form of a certain Presidential candidate, we may have hailed in public the rise of a statesman, but we were thinking in private that almost anything might fly. Nobody ever looks inside a Senator to see what makes him go; it is explained by Indiana's utter carelessness or Rhode Island's absence of mind. One does not ask his boots how they climbed upon the mantel-piece; one knows in heedless times that things get out of place. A Senator is merely a sign of other people's inattention. We may be a little careless in our language, but in private life we no more believe in the rationality of politics than in the rationality of success. Prodigious financial intellects are not much admired privately. They are, indeed, exceedingly uninteresting. It is only a magazine writer who can see the signs of power in that financially successful face. In private we merely see that it looks a good deal like a walrus, and from what we know about the man

himself we have no reason to think that, apart
from financial emotions, he did not feel like
one—one corner of the mind spidery, organis-
ing, grasping detail, all the rest pure walrus.
In public we say the race is to the strongest;
in private we know that a lopsided man runs
the fastest along the little side-hills of success.
Mothers still punish their little boys for the
winning ways of the rising statesman, and there
is seldom rejoicing in any home when a decent
all-round baby begins to decay into something
like a Harriman. In private life these remarks of mine are platitudes; in public thinking they are really quite profound. Approach
them by way of "social psychology" and you
will feel that you have penetrated far.

Nor have we in private life any such faith
in the rationality of political reformers, as
might be presumed from our magazines. For
some years past we have had a chance to ob-

serve closely an unusual number and variety of reformers. It has been a period, some say, of moral awakening, though as I look back upon it, it seems rather a period of journalistic fits and starts. For it was the era of those strange magazine early birds, known as "muckrakers." Many could understand why a muckraker chose his subject, but few could explain why he let it drop.

Apart from any moral consideration, the sudden cessation of many of those interesting magazine exposures was, I think, a literary injustice. A picaresque romance of gangs and bosses would run through three numbers of a magazine, then stop as suddenly as a trust prosecution. I acquired at the time quite a taste for corrupt aldermen, but the means of gratifying it were soon abruptly denied. What ever became of those interesting rascals? And how fared it with St. George and the Dragon

—and that affair between Ormuzd and Ahriman (pronounced in the magazines Harriman), how did it turn out? Often the best things happened after the serial had ceased. That much I could gather from newspaper despatches (tantalising bits, no real story), but search as I would I could find no magazine narrator resuming the thread of his plot. The final " graft " trial in San Francisco had, for example, according to the newspapers, a court record of four million words,—a mine of " vital human interest," moral throbs and devilry, better material than went to the making of the whole San Francisco corruption magazine series down to the day it stopped. Assassination, suicide, perjuries and plots, theft of documents, bribing and out-bribing, corruption never so thick, lying never more ample—what more could one wish? Yet not one good consecutive magazine story of it during the year—

San Francisco's best year for literary purposes. Observe that this criticism is merely literary. Let others take the civic measure of those magazine reformers, early moral minute-men, muckrakers, demi-socialists, whatever they were called. I dare say it may have been reform, for all it looks now so much like flirtation. I blame them here only as traitors to the common curiosity, who from having overdone many beginnings cheated us out of some very interesting consequences.

And what befell the reformers themselves? Apparently the republic has forgotten even the names of many muckrakers, quite famous in their time. No one seems to know what they have been doing since. Swallowed up somewhere in popular magazinedom, deeply absorbed doubtless, but in what diverse things? It is an idle speculation, but I have often tried to figure to myself what some typical muckraker has probably been up to since "graft" became obsolete for magazine uses, though lively enough elsewhere. I can guess him only from his magazine's contents. Perhaps he was caught first in that timely balloon ascension. Perhaps he took a turn next with the negro problem or with Abraham Lincoln when those two topics plunged again into the "public eye." Perhaps the Emmanuel Movement drew him. Call anything a Movement and he would be likely to try and run with it a little way. He must have made several dabs at Prohibition as it fell in and out of the "public eye." The accident to the "public eye" occurs, by the way, very systematically in popular magazine journalism and must not be confounded with the burning of questions. A "burning question" may not appear for two or three numbers, and it seldom burns for more than four; whereas the "public eye" is continuously get-

ting people and things in it, being an aston-
ishingly open feature that never blinks for man
or insect. Probably most muckrakers went
straight into public eye work, taking things
just as they came—aëroplanes, poets' birthdays, the direct primary, benzoate of soda,
woman's suffrage, war on house flies—happy in
a variety that conformed to a natural coquetry
of intellect. A few deeper natures preferred no
doubt the slower round of the " burning question "—Is New York sufficiently religious?—
How about a college education? Even this
seems giddy enough. Fancy a life that hangs
precariously on the first blushes of " burning
questions," if I may mix a few figures of
speech. Think of the danger of becoming in-
terested, of carrying last year's enthusiasm
over into this, of the hair-breadth escapes from
last month's deepest convictions. There is always the risk that a man may retain some ra-

tional continuity of interest, utterly out of place in a popular magazine, likely, indeed, to wreck it. An ex-muckraker must have successfully dropped at least fifty subjects within two years just in the nick of time to save their becoming food for reflection. As I said before, I do not know the life, but am merely guessing at it from the magazines. It seems a hazardous sort of intellectual wild-life not without a curious interest. It is odd that no one should have thought of tracing the course of some muckraker since he disappeared.

But cock-crow journalism has at least a cheerful meaning to those who practise it, endowed, as they doubtless are, with temperaments of tough fibre and good spring, dominating routine, disguising perfunctoriness, looking forward to new subjects as to meals, sure of an appetite. Nor can it be denied that a buoyant enough mind may experience all the excitements of epoch-making, even when merely taking

CONSTRAINED ATTITUDES

notes on the accouchement of the present moment. And if there is no great zest for the present subject there is always the joy of escaping the one before, and above all there is the sense of motion, of new births, new dawns, new movements, signs of the times, moral awakenings, sentimental earthquakes, and the general mountainous parturition of the mouse-like little particular. Not such a bad life after all —perhaps as good as journalism has to offer —and if one could by wishing transform himself into a successful writer he might do worse than change places with one of these same volatile reformers, punctual seers and quick forgetters, who can always have an early morning feeling, no matter what the time of day— glad hearts bursting with important moral announcements, like canary-birds whose song hails with an equal rapture the breaking of day and the running of the sewing-machine.

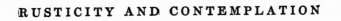

RUSTICITY AND CONTEMPLATION

III

RUSTICITY AND CONTEMPLATION

SENSITIVE folk, who shudder at the bustling "modern spirit," majorities, millionaires, motor cars, popular fiction, Sunday newspapers, imperialism, giant strides, nervous tension, machinery and like matters, who think the love of beauty dead or dying, art on the wane, "Culture" a forlorn hope, and taste commercially tainted, might take heart if they would look about and count the equally sensitive noses. They are a minority, to be sure, but a lusty one and exceedingly voluble. Consider the journalism of gentle contemplation. I have lately read more tender little open-air reveries, praises of Nature, praises of the soul, primrose reflections, shy musings, upland dreams than I could mention, some of them in books, some in the magazines, but many of them in the newspapers, even the coarse, pragmatical, money-minded newspapers. The journalism of gentle contemplation has become a profession in itself. Consider the remarkable increase and multiplication of good little Professor Woodside alone. Add to the books written by Professor Woodside the books that might as well have been written by Professor Woodside; add to these the woodnotes and general reflections of all the periodicals, especially the quiet thoughts of British periodicals about friendship, eventide, charity, an old churchyard, downs, lanes, hedgerows, wild violets, choughs, rooks, rabbits, or a sunset—and the murmurs of quiet meditation will swell to something of a roar. For literary seclusion is wonderfully prolific and Nature has, these many years, been almost mobbed for rustic notes. They are

44

formidable in numbers and of an amazing unanimity, these fugitives from vulgar modern majorities.

There are hundreds of them writing as one man, and they are read by hundreds of thousands—very naturally, too, for the subjects are altogether amiable and the writers' intentions good, and we are glad in this kind of writing to take the will for the deed, thankful even for the bare names of pleasant things. They alleviate the advertisements, financial articles, leading articles, and book reviews. " Brook trout " sounds grateful after " rate of exchange " or " brokerage," and it is pleasant to turn from the man who has unmasked the designs of Germany in Mumbojumboland to the man who has removed four large stones from a hill-top and uncovered a stormy petrel sitting on her eggs. But the stormy petrel man is far prouder than his brother of Mumbojumboland. His " feeling for Nature " does not extend to that hard-worked person in the next column, who is plainly just as much a fellow-creature as a coot and ought to be as interesting as a moor-hen, and who if turned loose with a note-book might do as well by " Nature's secrets " as he does by those of the Great Powers—know when a thing is bosky and when a thing is lush, know the wonderful hour that is neither night nor day, and the tang of salt air, and the skirl of the haw-bird, and the booming note of the dugong, and where the bumbleberries cluster thickest and the wild pomatum blooms—do as well by outdoors, in short, as the haughtiest of Nature's tuft-hunters. That is the vice of rustic and contemplative journalism—arrogance and the proud sense of personal rarity.

" The only unity of a Diary," said one of them in the Dedication of his *Diary of Tender*

Thoughts, "is the personality of the Diarist." It was not in the least a diary; nor had it any personal mark upon it. It was a volume of trim little papers about many charming and beautiful objects, pictures, books, the nightingale, daffodils, the sea, and clouds—essays in gentle emotion and appreciative observation which appeared in British newspapers and magazines. It is a gentleman-like and desirable form of professional activity, but as devoid of "personality" as any other kind of journalism—for example, the market quotations. Professor Woodside, also, insists firmly on a "personality," convinced that a certain smooth, sweet, even fluency in praise of quietude, flowers, brooks, the countryside, beauty, art, the ways of God, and resignation, is all his own. Yet no man ever stayed so long alike as Professor Woodside's manner. Each one of these many writers seems to think that when he has achieved a monotone he has expressed a "personality." An odd illusion, when one thinks how rarely "personality" appears in print. There is "personality," I suppose, in the descriptive writing of Meredith and Hardy, but that is literature. In literature men have the luck to be born singly; in journalism they are sometimes born in litters, but more generally are incubated in very large broods. The journalists of gentle contemplation are valued for their vocabulary alone. Personally they are undistinguishable.

I wonder if appropriate terms arranged in lists as in the spelling-books and followed by some single consolatory sentence would not serve almost as well. Thus—

Moor	Tender green
Heather	A glint
Bracken	A shimmer
Gorse	Bathed in sunlight
Curlew	Thrush singing

48

CONSTRAINED ATTITUDES

Lark	Lonely
Lazy clouds	Freshening breeze
Purple shadows	Lengthening shadows
Golden haze	One by one the stars
Distant chimes	Long-drawn sigh
A hush	Nature breathing
A cow	Vault of heaven

And as I made my way slowly homeward through the deepening gloom, it seemed as if some vast and mysterious but friendly power had strewn the soft, dark mantle of forgiveness over the world of struggling men and were whispering tenderly of peace.

I have found far more loyal Nature-lovers in the suburbs than in these literary wilds, and I know of a better sort of rustic journalism. I once read, for example, an excellent magazine called *Suburban Days*, which addressed itself exclusively to the class known as " commuters," that is to say, men of the monthly ticket, same train morning and night, indomitable, amphibious, never a night in town. It was not meant for your ten-trip ticket opportunists, who, as is well known, fall into a lax and desultory suburbanism incompatible with sound commutership, but for the men of the iron schedule, who do the deed twice daily, come what may. They alone, for example, could appreciate the sketches of prominent " commuters " who had won fame at one end of the tunnel while dining successfully every day forty miles from the other end. Careers of that sort are always heartening to a " commuter," teaching, as they do, that home may be attained each night and at the same time something else accomplished. Such lives shine with a double radiance, when there is something heroic about merely reaching home.

Hence the peculiar pleasure of reading in *Suburban Days* about a famous " comedian and commuter " (the wonder of his being both!) and seeing a picture of his lawn and learning that he raised chickens, which he " dearly loved." The love he bore those

50

chickens marks him as a true " commuter "—
who is always trying to raise something on the
place, and whether it be a hen or a young onion
it is dearer to him than to other men on account of the recurrent periods of enforced absence. Continuity will often cool the love of
chickens, but in a " commuter's " life of bright
renewals and extremely sudden cessations the
feeling never loses any of its early warmth.
And so it is with Nature generally, despite the
sneer of a recent writer that the " commuter's "
" return to Nature is only half way," and that
he lacks " the perspective of robust rurality."
No man rushes upon Nature more madly than
he or when torn away plucks from her a greater
variety of little keepsakes, bouquets of chick-
weed, boutonnières of beet tops, as may be seen
on any morning train, proofs that if the re-
turns to Nature are brief they are at least passionate. Your professional Nature-lover, who

mails his manuscripts from her bosom, could not find her in the suburbs at all, but the " commuter" can, the keen old zealot of " the wild." He noses her out somehow and has as true a forest feeling out between the clothes poles and the hedge as many a man living in the utmost literary wildness, strewing the dry bed of the mountain torrent with the galley proofs of his " robust rurality." There is the song of the river in his garden hose, and he is as clearly Nature's own as Professor Woodside beside his trout-stream. And do we love him any the less for his greater reticence?

And *Suburban Days*, being a well-edited magazine and true to its policy, saw to it that each biography of a great " commuter " should refer to time and distance not as obstacles but as blessings, for that is the brave tradition of the tribe. They give him a chance to read the morning papers—those sixty golden miles—

and even to run through the magazines, and
he usually gets a seat, and he is always there
almost before he knows it, and the time from
the front gate to the office door is never the
two hours of daily fact, but the hour and a
half of generous faith or some single tender
memory. Some of his most careful work has
been done on the way. If a writer, some of his
best thoughts have come to him on the train.
Privately I may say that every time a thought
of any kind has come to me on the train, an
umbrella or a handbag has somehow floated
away, but as a " commuter " I should not mention that.

THE HUMDRUM OF REVOLT

IV

THE HUMDRUM OF REVOLT

I BELIEVE Hedda Gabler is generally regarded as the most disagreeable of all Ibsen-kind. She has been violently assailed and with equal violence "interpreted" any time these twenty years. In spite of the attacks and the even deadlier explanations, the play has been several times successfully presented on the American stage. I have happened to see it only twice—once with a native actress scolding vinegarishly in the title rôle, and again with a Russian lady singing approximate English and inventing a character of whom Ibsen had never dreamt. Nevertheless the words of the dramatist were there, and they spoke for themselves through all disguises, holding the interest of friends and foes alike, Philistines and illuminati, the people who thought they knew what he meant and the people who did not care. No doubt the excellent gentlemen who were the most vituperative in the capacity of critics were the most enraptured as play-goers. For a gift like Ibsen's enlivens these jaded folk far more than they are willing to admit. Deeply absorbed at the time in the doings of the disagreeable characters, they afterward define their sensation as one of loathing, and they include the playwright in their pious hatred, like newsboys at a melodrama pelting the man in the villain's part. It comes from the national habit of making optimism actually a matter of conscience, and denying the validity of any feeling unless it is a sleepy one. Conscience, it would seem, is a moral arm-chair heavily upholstered.

CONSTRAINED ATTITUDES

Now, of course, if a man's own wits are precisely on the level of the modern American and English stage, there can be no quarrel with him for disliking Ibsen. If there is no lurking discontent with our stage and its traditions and with the very best plays of Anglo-Saxon origin produced in this country during the last twenty years, an Ibsen play will surely seem a malicious interruption. What in the world has a good, placid American audience to do with this half-mad old Scandinavian? He writes only for those who go to the theatre to be disturbed. Instead of beginning with love in difficulties and ending with a happy marriage, he begins with happy marriages and ends with the very devil. Considering the unerring sagacity with which all good-looking walking gentlemen select their wives, this is nothing short of blasphemy. And where are the signs by which a plain man may tell the virtues? The bloom of innocence is not the mark of a pure soul, but of no soul at all. The more respectable a character, the more apt he is to drive somebody to suicide. There are no villains to hate. Hate centres on entirely blameless people, who do their duty and break no commandments, on good husbands, God-fearing parsons, leading citizens, and the like —safe, practical folk living within the law and having the goodness that gets on in the world. The vices, according to Ibsen, are often the highly successful moralities of the moment, and the virtues are seldom quite respectable. He is concerned with good and evil as purely personal affairs, for which there is no recipe in any moral cook-book. He assumes that everybody has his own little moral workshop.

All of which seems commonplace enough to those who remain to some degree *feræ naturæ* —that is to say, a bit restive under social imperatives, or at least mildly inquisitive toward the totem poles of the particular horde, clan, phratry, "better element," world power, village congregation, club, class, home circle or moral chorus, wherein they find themselves imbedded; but it is very baffling indeed to the peaceful groupthinker. Nothing so makes a man's head spin as to detach his mind from the social mass with which it has coagulated in his middle age. And the twinge of an unused spiritual muscle is generally defined as a prick of conscience. There is no doubt whatever from the point of view of the best families, the solid citizens, those "whom the nation delights to honour," and the "backbone of this republic," that the spirit of an Ibsen play is immoral, indecent, perverse, and morbid. It was his purpose to have it so. Indeed, people are not nearly so uncomfortable as he meant them to be.

CONSTRAINED ATTITUDES

But to return to the ignominious chronicle of Hedda Gabler, that needless Norwegian young woman who, after five acts in demonstration of her superfluity, commits suicide at the fall of the curtain. No character to speak of, no respect for the gods of others or power to make a god of her own, a few appetites, but without will either to gratify or to subdue them, hence buzzing with little discontents and self-pityings in foolish maladjustment to the predestined pint pot—she is like, well, almost anybody at some stage of life, and like a good many quite ordinary folk all through, except that she killed herself, while they, with no more reason, go on living. To be sure, matters did seem rather desperate—married to Tesman, for instance, that utter doctor of philosophy, ashman of modern "original research," to be found in any American college catalogue. A single hour of him is bad enough, as every one knows who has met him anywhere outside a bibliography, for he is the product of that love for "German thoroughness" which never asks what the thoroughness is all about or what other faculty than memory the thoroughgoing creature possesses, but gives the name of scholar along with goodness knows what pink-lined hoods, doctorates, fellowships, chairs, stools, alcoves, and pedagogical perches to any academic beetle who gathers into shapeless little fact-heaps or monographs the things that a scholar would throw away. A life of incessant wiving and mothering of Tesmans (the lower academic organisms breed rapidly between monographs) might well stretch out in rather appalling eternities, especially to a highly strung young woman of the sort that demands much and gives nothing.

For Hedda lacked those impulses which help some women to pass the time even when they

have married Tesmans. She had not that fero-
cious nest-making passion which often serves
as well to keep a woman busy as romantic love,
religion, or the spending of money, and which
might have wreaked itself for forty years on
dusting Tesman furniture. Nor could she
throw herself, as women do in our own little
university Tesmanias, into societies of literary
endeavour, genealogical congratulation, sex-
patriotism; or move in solid phalanx upon the
works of William Shakespeare, cheered onward
by the pale but unscathed gentleman in the low
collar who had read the bard; or lead " the
literary life" (short stories with sweet end-
ings, full of "uplift," for wonderfully homo-
geneous magazines); or read papers at the
Woman's Auxiliary Annex of that local Sim-
plified Spelling Lodge of which Tesman would
assuredly have been an active member. In
other words, she lacked not only the heroism of

perfect domesticity, but the fire of parochial ambition.

Desperate as the case was, there might have been something to do had there been any heart for it, but Hedda was one of those *sub voce* insurgents who wait until insurrections become respectable—would have liked to murder Tesman if murder were in good repute, saw nothing wrong in adultery, but did think it impolite. She wanted firebrand joys, if only they did not raise the social temperature. She thought she had ideas of her own merely because she lacked the ideas of other people and would like to do a "beautiful deed," the measure of beauty being its distance from the standard of the neighbourhood. In short, she felt the glamour of the unconventional, believing even that an intoxicated gentleman, instead of being sent home in a cab by those whom he annoyed by his stertorous breathing, talked like an Horatian ode, or danced blithely, "with vine leaves in his hair," on a Grecian vase in bas-relief. So Lövborg seemed to her a man who lived his life, which he passed either in getting drunk or being petted by women for staying sober. He happened to bé a man of talent, too, but she cared little for that, valuing him merely as a fallen angel. But he, though glad enough to take Byronic advantage of any fallen angel point of view of any pretty woman, and liking the " vine leaves in his hair " and other euphemisms, turned for any real help in his work to another sort of woman, one less fearful of her neighbours' tongues. Hedda envied the other woman's influence, but would not have paid the other woman's price.

How to have a hand in Lövborg's life without doing anything for Lövborg, how to be a power in her little world along the line of least resistance? Well, she could at least keep him in his fallen angel state, and by encouraging him to drink and burning his manuscript show herself not altogether impotent for good or evil, and incidentally avenge herself on the other woman; and by urging him to a "beautiful deed"—that is, to kill himself—she could do something for the picturesque. Nobody need know, and her revolt against circumstances being a private affair, she would still be respectable. But circumstances shifted, and she must either figure in a vulgar scandal or do the bidding of an intriguing admirer, who had found her out. So she killed herself, following still the line of least resistance. Never was suicide less horrifying. So little of value was there in her that it seemed less like taking human life than like removing débris. Her soul, if she ever had one, had long since gone to the button-moulder.

CONSTRAINED ATTITUDES

And who is there for us to praise or blame and of what use is a play unless we come away praising or blaming somebody and reassured in all the sentiments we had about us when we first went in? Is the stage a place for sheer blank wonder why people live at all or why there are so many of them—like the piazza of a summer hotel? For this poor lady was beyond the nourishment of either the good or the bad. She had no heart for keeping the Commandments nor any heart for breaking them, and at no point can we say things would have been better had she done otherwise, but only if she had been resouled or reborn or not born at all. Therein she resembles a host of technically good and useful persons, save that she felt the tedium of personal vacancy, whereas they quite forget it in the dust raised by a thousand and one enigmatic social activities, buying and selling, despatching details, whirling around at the world's business of keeping the world as it is, feeling no private incentive whatever while pushed along by the little proprieties.

But if the law of other people seems not to fit one's own peculiar soul, it does not follow that one can flourish on the bald denial of it. That is the simple faith of the clever few, who, hating a crowd, think wisdom the mathematical converse of what the crowd thinks, and truth a negative adverb, and wit merely the longest perpendicular distance from the axis of the commonplace, and so, by taking a bee-line away from the obvious, arrive in disconcertingly large numbers at the North Pole of commonsense. They believe with Hedda that the beauty of the deed lies in its shock to the neighbourhood, confounding the love of truth with a sort of agoraphobia, substituting one formula for another, but living by formula, nevertheless. Surely people never seem so much alike as when at particular pains to seem different—witness the family likeness between men with long hair. It is as hard to find an individual in the most advanced group of devil-worshippers as in the Main street Baptist Church. It is not the size of the group or its moral code, but the extent to which it has digested you that decides the question whether your soul is your own. Pioneering spirits require a surprising degree of unanimity on their exclusive planes. Hedda was merely a mechanical dissenter. She might have been a brilliant essayist, paradoxical playwright, iconoclastic minor poet, if she had only known. But Ibsen killed her, thinking it perhaps the happier ending.

The lesson in it for me is that there is no lesson, and the pleasure of it is merely that of intimacy with a fellow-mortal, to a degree sel-

dom permitted off the stage, and never allowed
upon it by any modern English-speaking playwright who knows on which side his bread is
buttered. For years the allegorical procession
has trooped along behind the footlights, laudable characters beautifully rewarded, ladies re-
penting in the nick of time, knaves duly pun-
ished, tender babes, rugged cowboys of ster-
ling worth, brusque but well-meaning uncles,
wayward sons with hearts in the right place,
and wives either resisting temptation or yielding to it at their peril, and never one of them
having any life apart from their moral mis-
sion to me. As a play-goer I have done nothing but learn my lessons, and have seldom met
a human being, even a disagreeable one. As a
play-goer I have learned to be monogamous,
an upholder of the hearth, almost an andiron.
The theatre in the course of fifteen years has
taught me not to marry the adventuress, or to

pass myself off as the real heir, or to poison the lady's mind against my rival, or to speculate with my sister's trust funds, or to marry the wrong person before I know that the object of my affections is really dead, or to throw my life away merely because the letter did not reach me in the mail. I hate assassins and I give self-evident hypocrites a piece of my mind. I never run away with anybody except with the most honourable intentions. All this and much more I have learned as a play-goer, but as a person I have hardly ever seen another person on the American stage, and have no reason to expect that any practical playwright will ever permit me to do so. Hence the surprise and pleasure of the recognition—especially when it comes about through an unprepossessing old Norseman, shorn of all native charm by translation, unblessed by humour in any form, and expecting every man to bring his own philosophy.

But any resolute public thinker can some-how draw a lesson from it. Perhaps it is an allegory of the wages of sin. Or, if Mr. G. Bernard Shaw is your mental executor, you will certainly see in it " humanity outgrowing its ideals." Or may Hedda not symbolise the undoing of the artistic temperament, as an-other interpreter has shown? Or the duty of adultery? Or suicide as a pardonable manner of exit from married life with a doctor of phil-osophy? Then there is Mr. Roosevelt—is she not a plain warning against letting the heart stray from the home? And the Prohibition-ist platform—had not Lövborg drained the fatal cup, Hedda might be living to this day, the mother of nine little Tesmans. For this old inquisitor-general of all the formulas is forthwith translated into many formulas, and by the strangest of ironies it has come to pass that the self-same Ibsen who cursed people for not finding separate ways of their own now trails behind him a long and solemn file of "Ibsenites" in accurate lockstep with himself. So hard is it not to commend our souls unto our neighbours, or to live a life without forming a committee on the rules of living. It is a wonder that we still contrive to die personally instead of somehow getting ourselves collectively adjourned. And assuming the chance of a future life, consider the embarrassment of the sorting angels trying to pick out the personal particles as we arrive in our respective packages—schools of thought and squads of taste. Fancy trying to tell which, in any essential sense, is which, in a group of recent American novelists or business men, party leaders, " representative New Yorkers," successful playwrights, literary critics (by tradition), aristocrats by birth, aristocrats by reading Browning, or any of the other needlessly agglutinated bundles of public-spirited, public-opinionated, privately disinherited ghosts.

To be sure, the spirit of an Ibsen play, if once revealed, would be very disconcerting to many settled minds. It should be concealed, for example, from the tender millionaire and shrinking railway president and shy upholder of vested interests and all in whom the private moral and the public countenance are smiling twins, and perhaps also from the " plain people," for, according to our editors and publishers, they are always very delicate, and most certainly from those whom the people choose, for any sort of new feeling might shake the very foundations of immediate success. But it is safe enough for terrible fellows like you and me, dear brother-scribe or fellow-failure, ravening among the flesh-pots of literary speculation, libertines of dreams, reckless of the modern writer at his fiercest, ready for any giant that may come out in the magazines, even though he eat us skin, bones, and moral sense, ready for the incendiaries of the imagination and regretting only that in these well-watered literary times the fancy will not burn. It is not for us to complain that any drama on the modern stage is intellectually upsetting, but rather that it does not upset us so utterly as we could wish.

In a book about anarchists which I read not long ago, the author either described or invented two characters which had Hedda Gabler's same power of suggesting analogies. He said it was a study of the temperament of revolt, and an attempt to make clear the natural history of anarchists. One of them was a girl of the slums, who became the mistress of a rhapsodical young anarchist with literary tastes. Her mother was half German, half French and often hysterical; her father was a German machinist and generally drunk. Sensuality, neurasthenia, a potential talent too weak to work, insatiable egotism given to what may be called auto-poetry or self-crooning (private lyrics of one's peculiar soul not necessarily musical but imagining a very musical applause), and above all much hit-or-miss reading of writings reputed extreme—and you have the heroine, or, rather, a considerable part of her, for she was too good a literary or natural product to equal any such bare list of qualities. One thing she certainly was not, and that is a mere anarchist. Her relations with the anarchist movement were merely incidental. Any excitable artistic male might have done as much for her soul as the anarchist dreamer with whom she fell in love, and "social rebel" is too narrow a term for such an epicure of emotion.

For her, as for Hedda Gabler, humdrum

was the enemy, not "society." When anarchism became humdrum she took to the
woods—went into a camp in California,
where the author finally leaves her, "making
a last effort to live the straight free life of
Nature's children, a suckling at the breasts of
Mother Earth," and quoting from the writings of Professor Woodside, the Nature-
lover. A new birth, he calls it. A new appe-
tiser, the reader says, and wonders how the
feelings are to be scraped together next month,
though quite sure that she will get them somehow. The author seemed blind to the amount
of yeast he had put in her. He seemed not
to know that she was blessed with enough
power of self-dramatisation to last a life-
time. It was absurd to assume that she would
stay long with Professor Woodside and Nature—small blame to her, for far less restless
souls than hers have fretted under that com-

pulsion. It was absurd to assume that she would stay long anywhere. The author tried to teach a lesson by her, but she became too real a person to stay inside his proposition. That is the danger to the thesis-writer of drawing a character too well; it walks off on its own feet, snapping its fingers at the author's educational intentions.

It is proof of some power in a book if it sets one to speculating in this way, hunting analogies, exceeding the author's apparent design, and interviewing the characters on one's own account. The pleasant clever novels of the day leave no such illusion that the characters have got away, and give no such impulse to a wildgoose chase. It is a strange man that could remain awake five minutes beyond his usual time with any of the persons they describe. Gone like a glass of soda water; cheerful but done with; as ancient and hazy after two ticks of the clock as Tiglath-Pileser; and the soul now ready to be completely absorbed in the deeds of the flies on the window pane.

Her anarchist lover talked incessantly out of books with frequent allusions to seismic souls and Cosmos. It was the voice of literary youth, or of any man in a radical mood, called "modern" by reviewers who pretend not to know that radicalism is a ratio, not a creed, and may have been a constant ratio, for aught we know, since the first rebellious anthropophagus condemned the table manners of the best society. He said the world to him was a "halting hell of hitching-posts and of truculent troughs for belching swineherds."

He was the slave of the principle, no work without inspiration, and tramped and moped and starved rather than turn his hand to any task that seemed for the moment disagreeable. The disagreeableness of the task was proof to him that it went against the freedom of his nature, was a form of social coercion to which he is anarchist must rise superior. To work for wages was to approve the system of exploitation. To work for applause was also base. One cannot be quite sure of one's motives. He must wait for a work impulse that should be self-evidently untrammelled and unalloyed, an autogenetic impulse, a sort of moral seizure; then the mind might work with anarchistic propriety, work because it really wished to, voluntarily up and dance, or be bowled along the line of no resistance. But there are often long intervals between these happy turns, for there is treason within us from the anarchistic point of view. The mind is already compromised; the thoughts are by no means free (some of them snub others): the reason is often browbeaten, and sneaking little conventionalities start up every moment and

81

run the intellect in their own way; clearly the mind has been altogether overrun by " society," the enemy. Hence waiting around for pure ego-work to begin, soul cries, self-outbursts, is apt to run to very long pauses indeed, for the harder one looks inside his head the more entangled it seems with " society." And as the muscles need the pressure of objects that resist, a mind thus denied all exercise is apt to become at first flaccid and short of breath, and then, a mere pendulous, foolish thing awaiting justification by galvanism. So our anarchist ran his course. He was very logical. He applied the principles of anarchism to his own mind, and with entire consistency in freedom's cause he let it go to pieces.

In his company the heroine plunged into indiscriminate reading of the brilliant writers of the time, some with wings, some with dubious flying machines of their own devising, but all essaying an upward and forward motion, skippers of tradition, and if not pioneers, at least fugitives from commonplace. She brought to them a mind without previous acquisitions and an experience almost exclusively physiological. So she became, like certain insurgent magazine verses, extremely vague as to the identity of her oppressors, sure only of her revolt. She quivered as she read like an unballasted reviewer afloat in some tempest of "strong" writing, in a Jack London gale, for example, with the words "primal" and "elemental" tearing through the shrouds. "Cosmos" and "cosmic," as her lover used them, would at times delightfully capsize her. She began her thinking in terms of enormous girth and unapprehended content. Her first ghost stories were of "society." She had a woman's very personal way with large abstractions, making enemies or pets of them, like the woman quoted by Professor James: "I do so love to cuddle up to God." She acquired that precocity of literary feeling which prompts to "confessions" in advance of thinking, and you will find her likeness in a great deal of the premature poetry of the present, written in a flutter of expectation over an idea that does not come.

No plodding for her. "Small hath continual plodding ever won, save base authority from others' books." But occasional plodding is necessary even for the epicure of emotions, to get up an appetite for the next sudden revelation. She read for the pleasure of feeling the thought jump, but without the acquisition of a good deal of dense traditional stuff there is nothing for the thought to jump from or over. Where is the fun in seeing Mr. Bernard Shaw knock ideas down if one has not first met them standing up? Apart from any question of truth, or character, or the "meaning of life," and merely from the point of view of sportsmanship, the mind needs its level expanses, studious trifles, sleepy acquisitions, dry details, traditional irrelevancies, statistics, tariff discussions, polite conversation, leading articles and mild ambling poetry, including many hymns— in short, must plod along rather diligently at intervals for a due sense of the length, breadth, thickness and perfect humanity of platitude, from which alone the rocketing may be enjoyed. Otherwise these hop-skip-and-jump fellows will seem pioneers from nowhere or insurgents against nothing in particular. Even as mere pleasure-givers they will pall, if one does not retain some laborious habits, remain something of a scholar in commonplace things. She wanted the emotions without gathering any material for them to act upon.

She lacked, therefore, the staying power necessary even to successful hedonism, could not stand the training, the abstinence, the exercise. One sees signs of her in all classes, not merely in the slums and not necessarily versed in anarchism. The most of her will perhaps be found in literary Arcadias, where, as they will tell you, they have " good talk." But she pricks the mind to seeking analogies in very respectable quarters, which must not be mentioned lest they seem far-fetched, or violate a confidence, or provoke a libel suit.

THE USUAL THING

V

THE USUAL THING

I suppose I should sadly miss New York's best Society if it ever vanished from our books. It is only in American satire and fiction that I shall ever visit those expensive places, where, as a distinguished novelist has recently said, "proud beauty hides its eyes on the shoulder of haughty commercial or financial youth while golden age dips its nose in whatever symbolises the Gascon wine in the paternal library." In Cornville, Massachusetts, where I now live, the people do not do such things. And I like to think as I shake the furnace down of nights how different those upper people are, and how remote from life's realities and coal-bins, and

89

especially how shallow, up there on the silly surface of the earth, compared to a deep person like myself, good old truepenny, down at the bottom of things, *tenax propositi* beneath the cellar stairs. Probably there are not two fine minds in that entire class, said the distinguished novelist. I like to doubt if there is even one good soul. Noodles and Jezebels, say I, the whole pack of them; and I like to think that the Cornville circle in which I move is full of plain people but profound, hearts of oak with no nonsense about them, or people of "Culture"—the real thing, not from Chautauqua but from Cambridge—or people at once instructive and blithe, giant minds at play, gay astronomers, bubbling palæontologists. And I like to look down from these people of my fancy on that other kind of people whom I do not know, and to hate the Persic apparatus and that symbolic Gascon wine, and to feel that

90

CONSTRAINED ATTITUDES

I am intellectual and *integer vitæ* and other things that money cannot buy.

So I try and cherish the simple faith, built on the writings of some sixty years, from George William Curtis downwards, that New York Society is made up, not of people, but of types, each with a moral meaning no less plain that the personages in *Pilgrim's Progress*. But it is not easy to believe in types as compounded by the usual writer—phrase-haunted, fiction-rooted creature that he is, athirst for moral contrasts—and it so happens that no unusual writer has ever written of our best Society. Your true novelist does not stop with type; he completes an individual, having some momentum of his own, doing or saying the unexpected thing, often irrelevant; and I suppose if New York had had a Thackeray or Meredith her fashionable folk might have seemed more probable. As it is we have only Mrs.

Potiphar, the Reverend Cream Cheese, the Settum Downes, Minerva Tattle, Timon Crœsus, and later their derivatives with hyphenated names, abstractions whose daughters marry English lords, metaphors who run away with one another's wives, Van This, a virtue, and Van That, a vice, and the sad tale of some figure of speech who lost all his money and then shot himself. In books the authentic Vanity Fairs all seem to come from foreign parts.

Exposed as I am to only potato-patch temptations I should like to realise these moral perils of our gilded halls, but in our native writings this is difficult. No story of damnation is complete without a man, and no writer on our best Society has created one. For the usual literary mind is, as is well known, lined with a kind of wall-paper, running a pattern not its own. Novelists do not invent or observe; they rearrange their literary memories.

CONSTRAINED ATTITUDES

Satirists borrow not only their scorn but even the objects of it. And surely no fashionable group is more subdued to precedent. They have their pen-fashions and their etiquette with goodness knows what literary gentilities, passwords, *cachets*, literary class distinctions, horrors of the unaccustomed, rules of who's who and what's what and the proper thing in heroes and the proper thing in thoughts.

A hundred years of precedent will rule the action of a woman's face, especially the heroine's. It must be a face in which the colour comes and goes—run by the literary signal service. Shadows must flit across it, smiles light it, horror freeze it, blushes warm it, moral indignation turn it purely cold. And not once will that ever-busy face swerve from its precedents. The novelist will not employ the comparatively uneventful human face; still less will he devise a face and run it arbitrarily to suit himself. I recall, to be sure, one character in fiction whose "whole face upheaved"— plainly an innovation—but she belonged to the self-willed Henry James, an anarch among novelists.

And considering how writers set about their tasks it may be unreasonable to expect any sort of lifelike consequence. A novel is not a product of imagination. It is the electic effort of a literary memory schooled by a social demand. Probably it is no more reasonable to look for human nature in a novel than to look for Nature in a woman's hat. Not, of course, to compare a great novel with any hat however admirable. That would be equally disparaging to both; one does not care to think of a work of genius as disappearing like a hat or of a hat as surviving like a work of genius; the thought of an eternal hat is even hateful. But between the hats of the highest rank and the novels of the second there seems to be a sound analogy.

For each being a work of customary or crowd-derived inspiration, their value in depicting life is much the same. One matches human nature as already published; the other matches Nature as already worn on hats. So with a host of virilities and vitalities, love-storms, moral whirlwinds, Ruritanias, calls of the wild —you never meet the novelist who first employed them. You see the thousand hats that followed the example but never the great, brave, strong, protagonistic and outrageous hat that set it.

The call of the wild as seen on women's hats some seasons past proved no wild fancies in the heads beneath them. It was a call to precedent. When you found on a hat some singular bit from wildlife, say a weasel sleeping on its native beads or biting its light blue omelette,

95

it was not a sign of any personal wildness. It had occurred on many hats before. And so with the novels then in season. The call of the wild in novels at that time was not a call to any special wildness; it was the peaceful call of one Jack London to another. The law of each craft is redistribution of the parts, and the law of each part is that it shall have appeared successfully in public not very long before.

And since obedience to these laws is usually unconscious, I have heard it said that the joy of the work is often not to be told apart from the joy of first creation. Here indeed the hat has somewhat the advantage, for women do sometimes more utterly let themselves go, feel more of that first, fine careless rapture, in a hat than the novelist does in his novel. And as to the rule that, The style is the man, though I am not versed in the equations of self-expression, I believe it could be easily proved that the hat is more exactly the woman. A novel always seems a form of self-concealment. Yet a woman otherwise quite subdued may suddenly appear in a hat that is all ablaze with feeling—no doubt imprisoned passion's single mad escape—and you sometimes meet a hot, infuriate hat, hardly venturing to look at the rabid face beneath, yet find there a countenance of great serenity. The riot of emotion had passed off in the hat, leaving the soul at peace. This is not true of novelists, who, on the contrary, seen in the flesh, show personal diversities in hue, texture, patterns, general design, degree of animation, not to be guessed from any of their books.

And considering, by the way, the firm commercial basis on which our books like our millinery so often rest, I wonder why writers are generally supposed to have no aptitude for practical affairs. I never could understand those protracted discussions which arise whenever a romantic novelist takes it very naturally into his head that he would make a good mayor of Jonesville. It is the practice on these occasions to treat the political aspirations of the American literary man in a scornful manner, to recall the fate of his predecessors and to exhibit the supposed incongruity between our belles lettres and our practical politics. So far from taking it as a matter of course that our popular novelists should fail in politics, I find it a subject not only for regret but for astonishment. They are a hardy, sagacious, business-like breed. They are predominantly civic and practical. They have as keen an instinct for what people want as brewers, hatmakers, or grocers, and they are aiming, unconsciously perhaps, at results as immediate and tangible. In no other country is there so slight a difference between the qualities of the popular novelist and those of the successful man of business. The successful romantic novel of to-day is of pure business all compact. Too little is said of the mercantile shrewdness that goes to the making of such novels and the publishing of them in the nick of time. Leaving aside any literary criterion, I hold that as high commercial qualities distinguish the authors as adorn any Senator in Washington.

And in denying literary qualities to the evanescent novelists of yesterday or to-day, we do but smooth away certain obstacles in their political career. It is well known that among men at large the word literary has a formidable and exclusive sound. Even the word book will frighten voters. We should devise another way of speaking of these things. When a popular writer runs for office, he should be referred to as a manufacturer of bibloids. Let it be once known how unliterary most writers really are, and there will be more of them in the Board of Aldermen. Of the novelists in this country to-day there are but two men whose talents are so essentially literary as to unfit them for political office. It is of course impossible to imagine a more unloved Assembly-man than Mr. Howells or a more scandalous State Senator than Mr. Henry James. In their books they have disregarded a popular mandate on every page. But our other writers are guilty of no such divergence. Who could find any Pierian austerity about them? Current literature is not a jealous god; nor does it breed unthrifty habits, or a visionary turn of mind, or levity, or a too personal view, or any other spiritual twist that should disable a man's politics. On the contrary, success in it often proves a man possessed of the politician's greatest gift, the instinct for majorities.

Obvious as these analogies appear they escape our critics every day. Literary criticism mainly consists in judging each ordinary man by the rules of a different game from the one he is playing. Hence the servilities and hauteurs of those strange propounders of unnatural certitude, the literary periodicals, their hot and cold fits, false starts and stampedes; praise for the plodding author as if he were an artist, curses for him merely because he is not. A critic is commonly a person who reads with an unusual show of feeling some very usual book, then tries to turn the writer's head completely or else to take it off.

I read last week in the London *Bombardinian* that Robinson and Aristophanes are very near of kin. To-day I learn from the *Weekly Icha-bod* that Robinson in contrast to past glories

101

is the vanishing-point of the human mind. Yet Robinson could not have caused these persons this excitement. For Robinson is compounded of the very tissues of routine, and of like substance with many Browns and Joneses, and the mind that could not survey Robinson with composure would be shattered in a single day's experience. It arose, of course, from false analogies. One dragged in masterpieces merely to light up Robinson; the other to cast him in the shade. On reading Robinson they allowed themselves to think of literature, so horrid comparisons shot into their heads; whereas had they been thinking of more usual things, of hats, cigars, newspapers or their daily meals, they might have shown him in his true relations.

And since with a few exceptions here and there, the siftings of some centuries, writers do not report credibly of one another, or of any man, or of what they see or what they feel, but are m*h of a borrowed gesture, custom-pushed, too close to the world to give an account of it, it is rash to judge any city or class or group, or hang any dog on their evidence. That second simplicity which our best Society has not attained is certainly not to be found in the books about it. And in this good-natured land of easy prizes and quick forgetfulness with so much room for mediocrity at the top, climbing the Society ladder does not constrain to any more uneasiness of pose than climbing the literary one. They are not a care-free people, those " Cultured " few. Little of devil-may-care aristocracy about them; on the contrary rather a painful consciousness of status, it would seem, with need of very frequent explanations, mention of acquaintances among the proper set of books, display of credentials, proofs of *au-fait*-ness, proofs of *comme-il-faut*-ness, rebukes of the vulgar, snubs

103

for the illiterate, drawings of "the line," in short all the fidgets of the higher plane. The most respectably furnished intellects of our time often seem no more at home than Mr. Potiphar with his ormolu and black walnut. Nor was Mrs. Potiphar's grave concern for London liveries and footmen's calves more typical of fashionable Society in that day than of the prolonged colonialism of American letters, both in that day and in this, and including the *Potiphar Papers*. Our books, like the lives of our millionaires, show minds prostrated by their acquisitions.

Hence on reading some bitter little book about our best Society, I cannot feel as superior as I could wish, but must needs be thinking that it applies as well to a good many other grades and groups, composed of the ordinary time-serving sort of men, and perhaps to the author and perhaps to Cornville and to me.

And I wonder if he could have written so cynically of those fashionable goings-on, had he attended that last meeting of the Cornville School Board, for though it is not wealth or idleness that has spoiled us, it might have shocked him all the more to see how spoiled we are. Those who satirise some single group of us seem strangely merciful to all the rest. Those bitter persons do not know that their quarrel is with commonplace or realise how long that quarrel is.

I fancy if by some strange chance a wise man were to find himself amongst us nothing would surprise him more than this contempt of us quite ordinary folk for one another, class for class and group for group, the man of books for the man of dollars, each strutting among his misused opportunities, the humdrum critic for the humdrum author, mechanical poets for mechanical engineers, and the rank

and file of stage reformers for the rank and
file of plays. For he would see us for the men
we are, the sort that perish utterly and leave
not a trace, and would marvel greatly at our
imaginary inequalities. And I fancy he would
drive us almost mad by prying into these distinctions and by his superstitious talk, appeal-
ing to some demon or some god as the source
of real distinctions, and to the need of some
moonshiny inspiration, without which we were
merely usual persons higgling with one another about the usual thing, trying to found
little aristocracies of taste on grounds of common failure, spiritlessly pretending polite concern in spiritual affairs. And by the time
this peering and Socratic person had reduced us all to lowest terms, wonderfully equal
in absurdity, and wrecked our intellectual hier-
archy, and shown that there could not be any
great diversity of rank in our pantisocracy of

middling intellects, we should be thankful
enough to the eleven judges who hurried him
off to his hemlock. A fitting end to his war
with commonplace, and served him right, for
he knew that it led to the kind of philosophy
which has been rightly called the "practice of
death," and that if he would only keep the
peace, he too, like us, might be "eating and
drinking in Thessaly."

Yet our scorn of common things does seem
rather absurd when we ourselves are in no wise
remarkable. And so do our attempts to frame
rules in advance for artistic greatness or to
account for its long delays. One of the first
things a critic learns from the manuals of
American literature, is to explain the sleepy
state of our drama and letters by their youth.
Such a young country, and with manners so
unformed, such vulgar, rich people, such un-
stable lower classes, how can you expect a work

of art? We have dull books because life is empty, and if now and then a fairly good one appears, it is thrown away on so crude a subject. Wait till we cease to be common, till we get a " background " with some ivy growing on it, till the rich are picturesque, and society is stratified and the poor are in costume and know their place—then it may be worth while for a genius to begin.

Here we are, some of us totally bald and some with long white beards, yet all of us far too young to deserve either drama or fiction. There seems to be a breed of critics who believe in the utter vulgarity of here and now, and refer every artistic failure to time, place, subject, social conditions, to anything under the sun but the quality of the writer's mind. Books on American literature are full of these elaborate apologies, and you might think that the brain of an author was some superior kind of squash or melon that could seldom be raised here for lack of the proper fertiliser. Still more depressing is the view that a writer's failure is due to the material, that any sort of human beings, fashionable or unfashionable, finished or unfinished, are to blame for the writer's lack of interest or unworthy of "subtle method and refined analysis" or any other good thing he or she may happen to have. Why try and explain our "flat unraiséd spirits" by the ingrained commonness of things or cheat the uninspired with the hope that had they a higher subject they might soar? New York is not to blame for the quality of the books about her. You might as well blame Jerusalem for *Ben Hur*.

And even more absurd, I think, are our critical petulance and shabby excuses on the subject of the stage. Surely we might have spared ourselves our solemn trifling about the American drama these past ten years, discussing an art before the art emerges, bombinating in a vacuum, drawing disproportionate moral lessons from little foolish things. That is the bad result of applying artistic and intellectual standards to such matters merely to show that you have them about you. Later a sense of their irrelevancy comes upon you. They might as well have been applied to ten years of newspaper-reading, ten years of table-talk.

Compunctions for your own pomposity torment you in the intervals of self-approval. One of the cheats of the critical temperament is the belief that when its possessor is bored there is always some external reason to account for it. The critical person seldom admits that his ennui may be merely his own mind's little domestic tragedy. He reasons rather that it is a social disaster, sometimes of national dimensions, and the more he reflects, the more he

boils with public spirit, contrasting the present with the past and forgetting that the past
is a place where the little foolish things are all
forgotten.

If we had to be persistently intellectual and
analyse all the jokes into their constituents; if
the lines seemed like an almanac and the leading lady a little vulgar despite her good looks,
and the laughter irritated because we could not
share it, whose fault was it? Was it so very
different from the street or from any of those
large intellectually empty chattering-places
wherein men meet for purposes merely gre-
garious? There at least remained that glorious sense of superiority. How delightfully
few of us there were and how many of them!
Contrast the wit of *Our Flat* with the wit of
Hudibras, let the keen mind detect the lack of
logic in the plot, compare Charles Lamb with
Mr. Eddie Smith, and be cheerful in a splendid

111

isolation. There was no need of being crabbed about it. One could scarcely remain a patriot if he hated all fools.

After all, the lucky man of the present is he who can remain cheerful in the presence of the usual thing, when its only vice is its usualness. Reform often seems only the dislike of the blasé for the people with animal spirits. The oratory of ennui serves no purpose whatever. Ennui is a matter of reduced vitality or of spiritual defeat. It is a large, vulgar, garrulous and repetitious planet, and the play is only one of many human noises, not a picture of life, but an extension of it after all, and though our playwrights are not interesting as artists, they are at least objects of a reasonable curiosity as meteorologists of the public whims. I wonder if our warfare with these small matters will hasten much the coming of great things.

Yet I remember once seeing five musical comedies in a single week, always with my country's good in mind. It arose from a misunderstanding with a magazine. For some months past the London critics had been lamenting the overthrow of British drama by music, horseplay and the dance, and the question arose whether America was in like peril. So a magazine editor sent me forth to see, having mistaken me for a dramatic critic. I was expected to find something to say that would instruct the public, promote the general welfare, and tend to the improvement of the American stage. Wrapped in this earnest purpose I sat for five successive summer evenings through five musical comedies that were in all essentials just alike, and I did what the real dramatic critic usually does in like circumstances. I wrote as one who had " the welfare of the stage at heart." I complained that new musical comedies were not really new. I compared them with works of art and not with the products of industry. I had much to say about lack of originality.

Yet I knew that like other large industries the making of musical comedies proceeded on the principle of interchangeable parts. There was no need of a new musical comedy. An old one refitted with standard parts was equally serviceable. In fact, it is the purpose of a musical comedy only to seem new without being so—a sound business principle, as may be proved at any time by a study of soaps or tinned goods. As a biscuit-promoter, for instance, you would not aim at any large originality in design or novelty in flavour. An astonishing biscuit would not serve your turn. You would study the most successful biscuits that you knew and depart from them in no essential. You would con-

114

ceive your biscuit with a chastened fancy, viewing it as the pale flower of a public want, not as your private dream of beauty. taking the biscuit-eater as he is, not as he might be, and framing it on past biscuits tried and proved and still selling. As a biscuit-maker you would be self-subdued and un-Shakesperean, and your Butterettes would depart as little as possible from the highly prosperous Crispines, their predecessor. Your pent-up fancy would only emerge when it came to advertising.

The question we ask of the stage is only the question that we ask through life in this great iterative democracy, of books, of newspapers and of men—Why the same thing so often?

On returning to New York I have found in this artistic and literary sameness a sense of permanence that after a few months' absence I always miss in the streets. There at least I find assurance that I shall not fall behind the times. After all, the minds of playwrights and of authors are among the few remaining landmarks on which New York may surely count. It is hard enough in this city to preserve associations with any material thing. No indigenous New Yorker can revisit anything. No spirit of place for him. He cannot retrace the series of his homes. They have decayed into grocer's shops or shot up into apartment houses. His sky-line loses its teeth even as he looks at it, and in a few months from their sockets enormous fangs protrude. His university has zigzagged uptown, coquetting in the side streets, and is now perhaps for a moment pausing somewhere in the Harlem hills. Or maybe it is perching casually on the top of some tall building with a Latin sign—*perstando et præstando utilitati*, which in the circumstances sounds ironical. His club has dodged him five

times and swollen beyond all recogniton and
lined its fat belly with marbles and rich members and mural decorations, at which he looks
very hard and earnestly, hoping perhaps to
fix them in his memory before the house comes
down. But it is foolish to look hard at anything. It will only trouble him a little later
when he tries to remember where he saw it.
There is really no use in burdening his memory
with anything, except perhaps two rivers and
a sky. If his income increases and he wishes
to be fashionable, he moves northeast. If his
income increases and he does not wish to be
fashionable, he moves northwest. If his income remains the same, he moves from the
Plantagenet on this side of the Elevated Railway—which has raised the rent—to the Anda-
lusia on the other side—which soon will raise
it; then it is ho! for the Cinderella near the
water's edge. If his income decreases—but

117

there is no use in mentioning that, for to that extent he ceases to be a New Yorker; ceases, indeed, to be anything, fades, loses all meaning —gets himself perhaps a little ghosthood in the suburbs, but henceforth is never really anywhere, only on his way to it, a lost spirit of detachment, mere phantom of the to and fro. In any case he moves and in any case he cannot find the place he moved from.

But he will find the native drama precisely as he left it. There is always the new American play. Man and boy he has known it. It is one of his few old oaken buckets and ivy-covered things. Here twenty years are as one day and his neighbours are assuring him that nobody has grown any older. Why go back to the old farm and the dried apples and the trusty corn-popper? Associations with the play are even earlier—full indeed of a quite incalculable earliness. New York's tastes are her family antiquities and her familiar things are her new successes. She has no dear old woodshed and her hearths are like the nests of sparrows on a derrick, but she has new poems, as good as andirons, and new novels, such as one's mother used to read, and there is always a rising journalist, a rising dramatist, painted on the same quarter of the sky. There are few spots in her plays or her letters where one is not at home, almost too domestically. Hence to allay any perturbation on finding, say, after six months' absence, Fifth Avenue turned into a tunnel and my friends all gone beyond the Bronx, I have merely to see the play or read the novel. There is the *genius loci* in all its golden immaturity. After all, it is only physically and financially that New Yorkers buzz along. Our wits are at the old homestead. Therefore, when the critics fume as they do about our intellectual condition, let them at least for charity's sake remember that it is about the only thing to which New Yorkers may come home again.

IMPATIENT "CULTURE" AND THE LITERAL MIND

VI

IMPATIENT "CULTURE" AND
THE LITERAL MIND

I HAVE been reading a gloomy article in the *Didactic Monthly* by a professor of the social sciences who is sorry he studied Greek. He loves it, he says, but doubts its " cultural value " or effectiveness in the " battle of life."

" Would I trade my Greek," he exclaims, "considered both culturally and practically, for biology, for zoology, or for geology, let alone a combination (which would be a fairer equivalent) of these or similar other studies? A positive affirmative leaps to the lips."

He finds that his teacher fooled him about the classics, for looking back from his middle age he perceives that Cicero was conceited and Thucydides left clauses hanging in the air in a way that no magazine editor would now tolerate. The teacher never told him this, but now as a "reflective graduate he sees it and feels that he has been duped."

Of course, Greek should be better taught. Excellent Greek scholars, like eminent economists and sociologists, often seem strangely ill-nourished by what they feed on. That, indeed, is a frequent accident in the teaching profession—the teacher himself will often seem much damaged by his subject, no matter what the subject is. Educational writers are always blaming subjects instead of men, looking for some galvanic theme or method which when applied by a man without any gift for teaching to a mind without any capacity for learning will somehow produce intellectual results. It is a purely personal question and has nothing to do with Greek. It is odd that anyone should believe at this late date that any conceivable combination of geology, zoology, biology will save a man from these disasters. They happen daily at all points of the educational compass, in subjects the most modern and "culturally" vivacious, genuine "battle-of-life" subjects—pedagogy, potato philosophies, courses in sanitary plumbing, slum seminars in sociology.

"Gentlemen," says a voice from the past, " to give the full force of the Greek particles, which are really very important—very important, the passage should be rendered thus: ' Immediately as the troops advanced, the sun also was setting.'" It happens to come from the Greek class-room, but there are echoes from the other class-rooms quite as absurd, and, now that I think of it, this dried-up and belated old Grecian, long since dead, this eager and enthusiastic old gentleman whose spectacles leaped from his nose whenever he smelled a second aorist, was somehow more humane and less dispiriting, had made his learning more his own, liked it better, had better manners in imparting it, than the most modern and practical and pedagogically indisputable of them all. Greek did not give him these qualities; nor could the social sciences have taken them away. It merely happened that he was the kind of man in whom dead thoughts, whether in a Greek grammar or a government report, seem to come to life again; whereas there is no subject however "vital" that another sort of person cannot easily put it to death. Was there ever a "burning" question that could not be immediately extinguished by almost any one at an alumni dinner or in a magazine?

To be sure the present state of my wits is far from satisfactory and there may have been some magical combination, say, of botany, mechanical drawing, and palæontology, some grouping of studies, so divinely planned, so

126

" culturally " potent, that taken instead of Greek would have raised in me an intellect of unusual size and agility, a comfort to myself, an object of astonishment to visitors, but then again, who knows? Perhaps there was no charm in any part of the curriculum that could have wrought it; perhaps nature had something to say about it. In any event, is it right that a man on considering his head in the forties should blame Greek and an old gentleman twenty years ago for the state of it—write to the *Didactic Monthly* about it, complain that it would have been a better head if other people had not put the wrong things in it or packed it so carelessly that some of the things slipped out, or that it went by mistake to a Greek professor when it should have gone to some geologist? Maybe the face of Heaven was set against that head from the start. Certainly it makes a difference to whom it belongs.

It is one of the pleasures of growing old

and getting farther away from educators that we care more for the kind of head and less for the kind of facts that rain upon it, distrust all pedantic educational higgling over the " cultural " value of this or that, doubt the divine efficacy of any subject as a cure for the personal vacuities, doubt, when learned Greek meets scientific Trojan, which of the twain would be the worse to live with. And if a man has to go to middle age to find out that Cicero was somewhat conceited, Isocrates a trifle pompous, Quintilian rather inclined to platitude, it may have been merely a private affair, a secret between him and nature, involving no teacher or system whatever. For certain incipient activities may be expected even of the young. Was the young man waiting for artificial respiration? If Xenophon was merely a noun of the third declension who remarked to some people in the dative plural that either *thalassa* or *thalatta* was correct, if Tacitus was only a careless Roman who often dropped his verbs, obliging some anxious commentator to pick them up in footnotes uttering the startled cry of *scilicet*—even a change of subject might have done no good, for the young mind apparently had not yet emerged.

However, the literal-minded are they that inherit the earth, and if Greek literature or any other literature had really waked up this man's fancy, there is no knowing into what unsocial, unprofitable dream-corner he might have drifted, while progress buzzed past and problems whistled over him and education went fizzling by. He might have been a nympholept, for aught he knows, instead of a useful college professor, and spent days in mooning when he should have been up and doing, getting on in the world, educating, leading people from some place to some other place, no matter whence, no matter whither, but leading them. For it is a forlorn and pitiable thing in a democracy to go anywhere without taking other people— even through a book. Of what use is a citizen whose pleasures are private? We may thank our stars that we are born without imagination in these days or if we start with a little of it can easily kill it after childhood. It would be, I think, an isolating faculty in this democracy, unsocial, perhaps unpatriotic, a traitor to the sovereignty of the present moment, blind at a bargain, useless in reform, a heretic of social values, a sceptic of the scale of immediate importance.

An imaginative man might never read a newspaper. He could so easily invent more exciting news and more amusing editors. Imagining success, he might not want it. Imagining people, he might not care to meet them. Why should an imaginative man read a president's message or an opposition editor's remarks thereon, or hear the talk of a club member about either? Would not these novel and valuable forms of entertainment be staled in advance to that accursed and proleptic dreamer? He might soon be prefiguring next week's gossip and not reading .it, guessing at his compatriots instead of taking them by the hand, guessing himself so vividly in and out of public places that he would not wish to go. Many affairs of vast present importance would not be nearly so entrancing as a good quiet guess about them to an imaginative man. This is not the time and place for any praise of imaginative pleasures. They unfit a man for the travelled routes and main chances of this democracy. They encourage personal divergencies. They lead to conduct unbecoming in a social unit. They are neither civic nor aggregative, but split a man from his race, mass, class or group, by giving him secret diversions and absent-minded activities for which not a penny will be paid. They spoil him for an active part in any branch of that great society for the promotion of human homogeneity which under one name or another has been doing great work these many years in all parts of the country toward the obliteration of personal distinctions.

Hence it is better to read books as unimaginatively and impersonally as possible, thinking only of " results," of what may be turned to account, easily communicated, reduced to summaries, talked about, lectured on. Never a private taste without some form of public demonstration, if you wish to " get on in the world." And that is the safest way to write books, also, for an imaginative book is bound to seem a queer one. Readers desire that to which they are accustomed. They are accustomed to memory in a novelist, also to great mimetic skill and indust·y, but they are not accustomed to imagination. Accordingly they flee in large numbers from such a book, asking what it is "all about." That is one of the strange things about the literal mind. Why does it ask this question of books alone? It does not in the least know what the world is "driving at," but does not on that account run away from the world. It marries, eats, is fond of its children, votes, goes to church, reads the newspapers, slaughters wild fowl, catches needless fish, talks endlessly, plays complicated and unnecessary games, propels unpleasant-smelling engines at enormous speed along the road—all without looking for a reason or being able to find one if it did. It is at any moment of the day an automaton of custom, irrational, antecedently improbable, no more able to give an account of itself than a bit of paper swimming in the wind—but put a fantastic book

before it and off goes the creature indignantly
grumbling about the lack of an explanation.
As if the wildest thing ever written were half
so queer, inscrutable, fantastic or *a priori* incredible as the commonest man that ever ran
away from it.

We see more nowadays of this queer rage
that follows literary incomprehension because
there are so many more people who are trying
to read and write.   When an amusing and
fantastic little narrative was printed in England some years ago, I recall many stout Brit-
ishers who stamped on it with their hob-nailed
shoes, merely because it contained no large
round meanings like the *London Times* or Mr.
Crockett.   There is in these matters a sort of
loquacity of negation as if every one who could
not feel were bound to be a propagandist of
apathy.   The literary commentator seems
strangely jealous of the things undreamt of

134

in his philosophy. He is eager to vindicate his vacuum and the sequel to his " I don't feel it " is " Neither do you," usually with a show of ill-temper.

The theory of it is that all heads are of the same thickness and that the man who finds any meaning where you do not is probably an impostor. The excuse for it is the frequency of fraud, especially in literary cults. Cults as a rule are as soulless as corporations. One feels, for instance, toward certain uncritical lovers of Mr. Henry James as Emerson did toward noisy nature-lovers. " When a man tells you he has the love of nature in his heart," said he, " you may be sure he hasn't any." No one should be blamed for being suspicious of the literary cult. And it is as short-lived as it is deceitful; for it has been observed of its members, as of the blue-bottle fly, that they buzz the loudest just before they drop. Excesses of this sort have of late years been invariably followed by periods of severe repression—of silence almost proportionate to the degree of garrulity when the talking fit was on. The hush that settled upon *Trilby* and *Robert Elsmere* endures to this day. The reader of *The Man with the Hoe*, if there be one, is as the owl in the desert; and upon the lips of the Omarian the spider builds its web. Men still find pleasure in the writings of Stevenson, but where are the Stevensonians? Where are the Smithites, Brownists and Robinsonians of yesteryear? Let a subject once fall to the cult, let the lavish tongues of small expounders have their way, and the waters soon close over it.

But apart from this well-founded suspicion of the cult, there is no doubt that contact with the things that they do not understand is to many minds acutely disagreeable. All the greater dramas contain highly valued passages which are not only wearisome to many in the audience but actually offensive to them. A dog not only prefers a customary and unpleasant smell; he hates a good one. A perfume pricks his nose,—gives a wrench to his dog nature, perhaps tends to "undermine those moral principles" without which dog "society cannot exist," as the early critics used to say of Ibsen. Hatred of the unfamiliar is surely as common a rule as *Omne ignotum pro magnifico*.

But the great triumphs of the literal mind occur in the field of literary criticism, as when experts take the measure of the poets or tabulate their parts of speech. Consider, for example, the polemics of literary measurement to be found in almost any literary magazine. I never know which side to take in these discussions as to what constitutes true poetry or as to the relative measurements of bards. This is due, I fear, to gross inaccuracy. Parnassus has never been for me ringed with lines showing altitude above prose-level, like the mountains in the school geographies, nor have I been able to grade geniuses as accurately as I could wish. Ranging one bard along with another, old or new, great or small, I am apt to miscalculate by many centimetres. I am not even sure of myself in applying the Johnsonian parallel to present poets of a certain degree. I might say, for example, that, if of Bilder's Muse the steam pressure is higher, that of Barman is broader in the beam—but I should do so with little confidence that it would survive the tests of later investigators.

Hence my pleasure (a little mixed with envy) in many magazine discussions grading authors, according to sweetness, girth, weight, height, depth, speed and durability, with never a moment's doubt. Perhaps a compatriot of Emerson declares he is entitled to the first rank anywhere, and from this position shall never be dislodged, and a London reviewer says he cannot allow it because Emerson was lacking in *Je-ne-sais-quoi*-ness, and lived too long at Concord, Massachusetts, and much as he hates to disquiet America, he must rate Emerson two points lower. Or it may be that a visiting American Professor in the course of his Cambridge lectures does not rate the versatility of Dryden so high as it is rated by some Oxford don, who has scheduled the qualities of all the poets and marked them on the scale of ten, and the don turns quickly to his tables and finds that many of the Professor's tastes are inexcusably erroneous, wrong by Troy weight, wrong by avoirdupois, and that they are not always expressed in donnish language, several phrases being merely suggestive and three prepositions misplaced. So on this firm basis he proves the lecturer illiterate and shallow-pated, and then with wider sweep (for he happens to be writing in the London *Bombardinian,* whose policy it is to insult America as no grand division of the earth's surface has ever been insulted before) he dismisses all American scholarship as quite worthless and American.

Or, again, it may be that Mr. Barker (one of those rare expository poets, who after the printing of a poem can live handsomely for several years on the income of their explanations), appears once more in a magazine, and the question immediately arises, Is it a deathless song? And one maintains that Mr. Barker is the true bobolink singing with his breast against a thorn, and another disproves it by citing two or three

140

CONSTRAINED ATTITUDES

mixed metaphors or lines that he cannot understand.

> "The great white peak of my soul has spoken"
> "To the depths of my being below."

"How can a peak speak?" says the foe of Barker, but a man from the poets' ranks fells him with the Bible. "Why hop ye so, ye high hills?" says the Bible, and how can a "high hill hop?" And on they go, each deciding the thing absolutely and trying to bind the rest, and Mr. Barker waits cheerfully, knowing that his time will surely come, and meanwhile plans lecture tours along all the principal trade routes of the country. I may not address myself to these grave issues in the clarion tones that they deserve, but I appreciate the spirit of such discussions and like to see them going on.

Or suppose the great question of " English

141

style" reappears in the magazines. A sentinel of "Culture" has been found asleep; a professor of English literature in a book on rhetoric for the young has himself been quite inelegant. Thrice has he ended a sentence with the careless words "and so on," and on one page he has referred coarsely to "the business in hand" and on another he has said he "pitched upon a word,"—as if a gentleman would ever pitch on anything; it is the act of a drunkard or a ship. And thereupon some one all aglow with true refinement asks what our native language will become if men in such high station fall into blunders gross as these. And the blunders are then pilloried in italics or marched to jail behind exclamation points, looking very guilty indeed, and the newspapers copy, and editorial writers, straining to sudden dignity of phrase, comment on it with a splendid scorn. Finally, if the weather is

142

warm, "Typicus" and "Philologus" write letters ending either with "*Quis custodes custodiet*" or with "*Verbum sat,*" and others follow, and all concerned are soon debating whether you can be a perfect gentleman and end a sentence with a prepositon. It is a scene of great and cheerful activity, and no man with his heart in the right place will begrudge the participants any of their joy.

Yet it puzzles us simpler folk, who did not know that even the best of grammar could really save an "English style." For it is astonishing how vicious an "English style" may be without getting into the grammatical police court. And the man who writes about it at the greatest length on this occasion seems not to have attained it though he breaks no laws. ¯ The sentences are willing to parse for him, but that is all. They deny all complicity with his mind,

143

CONSTRAINED ATTITUDES

all ease, intimacy and sense of form; call up
no image and suggest no thought; do nothing,
in short, that might distinguish him from the
Comptroller of the Mint, the Board of Education, a Consular Report, or the Turveydrop
on the morning newspaper who took his treatise
as a text for a lecture on literary deportment.
Of course this is no fault of his, but in the ca-
pricious region of " English style " the personally blameless seem often to be the deepest
damned.   We forgive some men sooner for
breaking the law than others for breaking the
silence; and there is something about these
staunch upholders of the law that drives all
uncouth persons, like myself, to mad excesses.
We rush into some lonely shed and split in-
finitives.

And of what use is it to attack one Dr. Drybosh, as a daily paper did, because he wrote
six hundred pages on Tennyson's diction and

arranged the poet's idioms in classes and sub-classes and convicted his co-ordinate clauses of illicit intercourse? Dr. Drybosh is a mere pupil of the Drier Criticism, of which sad science masters are to be found everywhere, not only in college chairs of literature, but in newspapers, magazines, reading circles and women's clubs. Few people read a poet nowadays. They take a course in him. Some one arranges him first into an early, a middle and a later period. Somebody builds an approach to his " works " and somebody else a trestle over them. A Dr. Dowden may perhaps be found who will show how the buoyant tone of the poet's youth was tempered by the reflective note of his middle age. Then there is his relation to his time and to other times and the pedigree of his main idea and whether poetry had ever broken out in the family before, and, if so, why, and his likeness to somebody and unlikeness to somebody else, and the list of his ingredients, and how long they had to be stirred, and when they actually "came to a boil," and what his place was in literature.

True, Drybosh is a type much loved by college presidents, and rewarded usually with a Ph. D. (no mere ornamental appendage, but the indispensable prehensile tail for academic climbing), and often promoted to a special literary chair for dehumanising the humanities. But to be a Drier Critic, whether of the college chair or not, that is the best way to begin, and the Drier Criticism is at this day inexpugnable. For by means of it a man who has no heart for his subject may still draw from it his daily bread. Commensalism is by no means limited to bivalves, but runs all through the Drier Criticism. Shakespeare to his commentators is as the oyster to the oyster crab. The very definition of commensalism reminds one of the

146

latest essay on Browning or Walt Whitman; and why rebuke the manners of invertebrates, whether literary or marine? In all these matters one should strive for a more than human, an almost zoological, charity, and the hope that even a Ph. D. may have its use in nature.

Hundreds of naturally book-shy people, disliking the essentials of literature, are kept busy in its neighbourhood by just such tinker-work in its non-essentials; or they may at least be made to tarry near by papers on the " human side " of him, how the great man looked, wherewithal he was clothed, whence his thoughts came, and what he ate. I have before me a " Chat with an Author," profusely illustrated, and taking up the best part of a page of a newspaper. In the upper left-hand corner is the author's full face. At a distance of two inches to the right is his profile, the intervening space being filled

147

by a picture of a rose from the author's garden. In the lower left-hand corner is the author's front door. In the middle is a larger picture of the author, this time including his legs and the library table. In the right-hand corner is the library table again, but this time without the author, and below the library table may be seen an elm-tree belonging to the author. These are not the mementoes of the dead. The author is still living. The " chat " itself abounds in the same reverent miscellany. The author declares his preference for high ideals as opposed to low ones, and the interviewer jots it down. He breathes, and the interviewer notes it. A similar " chat " follows with another author, also " in the public eye," who supplies three portraits and maintains with equal firmness that high ideals ought to be raised and their seeds freely distributed. And so it goes. Scores of these literary interviews were appearing at that time, some papers making them a regular feature of Sunday or Saturday supplements. They were studies in effaced personality. Not a tumultuous or self-willed person at any time, the American author on these occasions faded completely away. He seemed a jelly-fish floating on the current of universal assent and owing his success, one would say from his remarks, not to any efforts of his own but to the country's willingness. It may have been the fault of the interviewer that he could detect in these authors only the qualities that are common to the race, and record only those sentiments which it would be a sin for mankind not to share. But I remember that one of them was made to say:

"The atmosphere in which ideals are found must be preserved to insure their accuracy, and atmosphere is the divine promise of ideals that the true artist finds wrapped around an otherwise sordid fact."

And the other interviews abounded in just

149

such comatose passages. Perhaps it was due to the benumbing effect of publicity. Just as many animals will not touch their food in the presence of man, so there may be authors who will not use their minds if they think anybody is watching them. Excited by the camera, and unmanned by the sense of impending advertisement, they are on these occasions not themselves, often utterly swooning away into the general morality. Later, perhaps, they find they have been saying that the world on the whole is growing better every day, or if it is not it ought to be, and that they do their best literary work between meals and with an earnest purpose, and that this is a great country, and culture clubs are dotting the prairies, and the atmosphere is full of ideals, plenty for everybody, so give the baby one. Which involuntary remarks, subjoining a scene of pillage, wherein their profiles, full faces and frock coats alternate with chairs, desks, tables, detached doors, bulrushes, twigs and other objects torn from the premises, constitute what is known as a literary "chat" published for the benefit of persons who might have taken grave offence at anything more intimately literary.

Apparently one of the chief objects of writing about books to-day is to entice these alien and reluctant souls into their vicinity and to comfort the aching hearts of "Culture"-seekers with the sense that "Culture" has been attained. Readers are seized in the midst of their reading with a mad Chautalkative philanthropy, and disdaining their own digestions, tell us what to read. I am constantly receiving advice as to my book consumption from people who look starved. "Culture" is always preoccupied with my conversion. There are writers for the London *Bombardinian* who have never read a line except for the discipline of me. In my own country there is the literature of the helping hand, more active than the Salvation Army. Unselfish men running back and forth all their lives between their books and me; devoted women telling me how to approach poets who are by no means fugitive; engines of literary "uplift," ably manned or womaned, from heavy, hoisting, academic derrick to smoothest of ladies' escalators; societies formed to make me feel as if I had read what I have not; road houses on the way to every well-known author for the pilgrims who never arrive. In England the duty which the man who has read something owes to the man who has not is tinged, to be sure, with a certain sternness. The Briton with a bit of literary knowledge in him makes it a class distinction, accentuating the ignominy of the man who has it not, pointing more unmercifully than we do to the horrid

152

gap between them—but always for that vulgar person's good. With us there are more who lend a hand or smooth the pillow. But common to this abounding helpfulness is the tendency to begin too soon. Too soon does the thought of others extrude all other thoughts. Too early and devotedly do readers plunge into the care of all minds but their own. The self-indulgent partaker is rare; the toil-spent, literal-minded, ill-nourished, eleemosynary book-executive or taste-commissioner is almost the rule.

I forbear to add any reflections of my own to the vast body of expository or satiric comment on this familiar democratic tendency, but I do protest against the view that even the most solemn of these missionaries are people who take themselves in the least seriously. There is no point in the common gibe about taking one's self too seriously. These people are swept away from themselves on waves of premature benevolence. In a humanitarian era they are clean gone into other-mindedness, having no private tastes, only ministerial inclinations, no personal pleasures, only social subsidiary utilities. These are not the cares of your self-serious person. The more seriously he took himself, the more lightly would he be apt to take the duties of this literary motherhood. He would leave us to make our way as best we might into Meredith or toward Dante or under Shakespeare or around Browning. No sign-posts from him, or guide-books, pathfinders, step-ladders, "aspects," "appreciations," central thoughts, dominant notes, real messages, helps to, peeps at, or glimpses of; in short, none of the apparatus of literary approach, and none of the devices for getting done with authors. For what should he care—that seriously-selfish man—about our propinquities and juxtapositions, our first views and early totterings? *Sauve qui peut* would be his feeling in these matters, coupled with no especial unwillingness to see us hanged.

A foolish phrase, that of taking one's self too seriously, and doubly so when applied to writers, accusing them, as it does, of quite incredible excesses—thinking too long, feeling too keenly, enjoying too heartily, living too much. And, as is well known, true literature is compact of very lordly egotisms, the work of men preoccupied with self-delight. Never a philosopher without his own first egotistic certainties, or a poet who was not the first adorer of his dreams, or a humorist whose own earliest and private laughter was not the nearest to his heart. Never a good fisher of men in these waters who had not first landed himself, taken himself so very seriously that we cannot mistake him for anybody else, maintained his egotism in a masterpiece—that most unblushing, self-interested device ever yet achieved for the preservation of personal identity.

LITERARY CLASS DISTINCTIONS

VII

LITERARY CLASS DISTINCTIONS

As a reader of current literary comment I have
often wondered why professional writers about
books love so dearly to snub one another and
me. I do not refer to mere phraseological
heirlooms from a pompous and didactic past, as
when it is said that "every schoolboy knows"
something that the writer has but recently as-
certained, or when the results of much grubbing on his part are introduced as "doubtless
familiar to the reader." I refer to the practice
of sniffing at a class of people whom he rates
very much beneath him—people on whom the
"subtle something" in B's writings is quite
thrown away, or who miss the "undercurrent
of philosophy" in C's humour, or who for some

159

vile canine reason prefer D to F. "No better touchstone of literary taste could be conceived," says Porphyrogenitus, "than ability to appreciate the following passage," and finding the passage spiritless and altogether mediocre I learn that I am of the canaille, and so would scores of his fellow-writers if all of them had not " touchstones " of their own whereby they in turn become Vere de Veres, banishing him to the butler's pantry. And the more respectable and British the periodical, the more hopeless the lot of the outsider, the blacker the unparochial outer darkness. Nowhere has the Proper Thing more awful beadles than in the unsigned pages devoted to "light literature" in the British magazines. For each is proud not only of what he does know, but of not knowing any more—*scienter nesciens, sapienter indoctus*, like the monk of old, or like Carlyle's gigman, if you prefer. I am always abashed before the British paragrapher, even when he speaks kindly of Poe or Walt Whitman or tells me Mark Twain is a genuine humorist. America lies so largely outside his experience and it is so clearly her fault and he is so grandly merciful to people who did not know they needed any mercy, and he is so very like one of his country's institutions and so very unlike a fellow-man.

"It would be churlish to deny," said an editorial writer for the London *Bombardinian* at the end of a severe rebuke of American taste in novels—"it would be churlish to deny that America has produced great writers who can hold their own with any European or Asiatic." Why "churlish," I wonder, and to whom? Is the country, then, so tender or the writer so Olympian that the cruel words must be withheld for fear of crushing? Would they not be

161

the words of a simple, harmless, unknown, pers-
piring man with space to fill and possibly a
printer's devil waiting and ideas hanging back
and no means of making sure of anything under
the sun and only some haphazard personal
tastes and private guesses to rely upon? Why,
then, that Atlantean manner, as if responsible
to the man in the moon for letting the world
slip?

Surely readers must understand the situation.
There is nothing papal about that well-worn
editorial chair wherein he wriggles, nor is he
by any magic transformed into an œcumenical
council, *vox populi*, enlightened public opinion,
consensus of the learned, fourth estate, moral
bulwark, or anything else more representative
or apostolic or numerous than a man with a
pen and an ink-pot. Nowhere, it would seem,
could a literary opinion be expressed with less
concern for the susceptibilities of nations than

in the unsigned pages of a British magazine.
Yet nowhere do words imply a more awful
sense of their own consequences. I presume a
man is actually not committing his publishers,
his family and friends, his country's institutions and her flag any more deeply by express-
ing an opinion in the pages of a British magazine than in the pages of an American book.
Yet here am I quite free and unconscionable
toward any poets or prose writers on the face
of the globe. It is not out of kindness that I
spare French literature, and I would as lief be
churlish as not to the literatures of England,
Spain, Germany, the age of Pericles, any country or any period, and may frankly tell them
the sweet or bitter truth—I like them, I like
them not. When I reprove a country's literature that country seems to know by instinct
that it is not her fault. Mid-Victorian British poets, post-Lincoln American poetasters,

Greeks, Romans, Scandinavians, whoever they may be, they ask no mercy from my powerful though undistinguished pen. Are they really in any greater fear of British weekliness?

But this approaches the character of Podsnap, and the actual, full-fledged British Podsnap, as you sometimes find him in the magazines, is a creature to be prized. I always clip and preserve his sayings, having something of a collector's mania for good specimens of the breed. Here is one that I have treasured:

"We question whether the time is not now rapidly approaching when it will be necessary for all sane and orthodox people to inquire of any new person that may be brought to their notice, 'Are you a Socialist or an Atheist?' and in the event of an answer being given in the affirmative to express extreme regret at being unable to go any further with the acquaintance."

Taking absurdity for absurdity, I never could see why the highly prized British types in comedy and satiric fiction were any more

164

valuable than many of these actual contributors to decorous British periodicals, for example, the *Hortator* or the *Bombardinian*. And what are they for, if not for the pleasure of a distant people? At home custom no doubt stales their exquisite pomposity. Probably the native Briton, subdued as he is to the respectable tradition, takes it as a matter of course that there should be scores of these anonymous beings episcopáting in an ink-pot, binding and loosing, delimiting the mind's permissible activities, dividing the earth by meridians of propriety, puffing up at the touch of an alien thought like a balloon-fish out of water when you tickle him. But in the more inquisitive soil of this country those large incurious Podsnaps will not grow—not, at least, the best of them, the genuine, full-bodied, calm, thought-proof, opinion-tight British ones.

I can no longer regard, said a recent writer

for the *Bombardinian*, I can no longer regard the Antipodes as a hopeful portion of the earth's surface. And there the matter rests. We shall never know what passed between him and the Antipodes—whether the Antipodes were wicked or merely careless, whether it was deliberate and personal or something impulsive and Polynesian, " so unlike the home life of our dear Queen." We know only that nothing henceforth shall pass between them. The acquaintance is at end. And again:

" We have been taken to task for saying that America was no more civilised than Japan."

And then, staunch old Podsnap that he is, he puts his foot down and says it again, and so settles the matter. Germany's turn next, and the Orient and the Tropic of Cancer and certain tribal doings of Africa, very ungentlemanly to say the least. No nonsense about Podsnap. He is not the man to shilly-shally with a hemisphere, and he does not mince his words. But if a continent behaves properly, Podsnap is willing to admit it. He is not narrow-minded, only firm. If, as Dickens said, Podsnap once disapproved of Asia, Asia at that time gave him cause, and since then he has had occasion to speak kindly of Asia several times. When Asia makes an honest effort to please Podsnap she is not repulsed. Asia under respectable institutions—House of Lords, London County Council—would find Podsnap ready to let bygones be bygones. He would do as much for America, though for the present he has dismissed her. Podsnap will forgive any grand division of the earth's surface that is truly sorry.

And who are these people that take Podsnap to task and would strip him of his opinions? If they are Americans, as some of them profess to be, they are disloyal to the spirit of their country. The land that restores a diplodocus, that would have liked to purchase Stonehenge, that actually imports Rameses and pays almost any price for an historic background, no matter whose; the country where few can afford to keep their own rattletraps so highly are they rated as *bijonterie*, where the keepsake is kept by some other family, and the soap-boilers of one generation become the vases of the next and the warming-pans its mantelpiece ornaments; the land whose young women may be seen at any time in ancient foreign cities ejaculating " Quaint " much as the duck quacks and telling the natives they are " dear old things," will always resent a retort upon Podsnap. For it is prompted by the desire to change him, and although that, luckily, is impossible, the wish to do so is none the less base. To remove an opinion from a certain type of Englishman would be an act of vandalism.

For the truth is, Podsnap, outside the printed page, is growing rare, which enhances his value to all who love to meet the things they found in Mid-Victorian novels. The crumpets are what they were; so is the ale; so is a cabman; but a man may traverse the length and breadth of the British Isles and never meet a genuine Podsnap. Indeed, the traveller brings back tales of a careless openness of mind utterly alien to Podsnap. Everywhere outside print are the signs of slackened fibre and a surface glitter of decay in the manhood that was Podsnap's. Even in print there are only a few publications to which the alien may turn with a reasonable chance of finding an absolute Podsnap. All the rest are honeycombed with knowledge and tainted with new-fangled relative views of things.

But this, I fear, is digressive. To return to more **purely** literary class distinctions: Even

169

when by accident my tastes are momentarily in
accord with some writer for the *Bombardinian*,
I cannot help feeling for the others, those vulgar others, "half-educated," "bourgeois,"
"suburban," who, say what you will, must
somehow be aware of their condition, and suffer
keenly. But it is given to no man to remain
long among "Discriminating Readers." Successive writers hew them down, till, if you follow literary journalism far enough, not one
soul is left to blush at the tale of his own ex-
clusiveness. It comes to the same anarchy in
the end, not only among the frank literary ego-
tists, men of "confessions," men of "para-
dox," but among the severest academic persons
full of grave discourse about the "best literary
traditions," recognised standards and the like,
speaking apparently for a class, yet each using
his scale of values as a personal step-ladder to
overtop the next. "In his treatment of Na-

ture," says the *Literary Palladium*, speaking of some undistinguishable person, "a prosaic thoroughness mars artistic effect." "As a matter of fact," retorts the *Weekly Rhadamanthus*, "precisely the opposite is true: A poetic thoroughness heightens artistic effect." And so it goes. Nor is it a merely rhetorical certainty. These strange creatures really feel all the absoluteness of pure mathematics or of childhood—and in regard to matters which in the long run will be ranged with millinery and waistcoat buttons.

The outskirts of literature, like the fringe of "our best Society," are full of these queer meticulous beings, concerned with Heaven knows what pass-words and cachets and easily horrified little gentilities—anxious debaters of what's what and who's who, and the minutiæ of precedence and the things one ought to seem to know and the ins and outs of literary table

171

manners. And the man who sips Walter Pater in old china must on no account be seen with the man who eats raw Kipling with a knife. And in the absence of any personal distinction there is this awful sense of class distinctions, conveyed in many shrugs and shudders and little screams; and books are neither loved nor hated; and " Culture" must declare itself or it would never be suspected; and you guess that a man is fully educated, because he calls some other man "half-educated" and seems to think it a very dreadful thing; and vulgarity is not a quality of the mind but a degree of literary information; and were it not for the exclamatory derision for the " half-baked " on the part of gentlemen who, presumably, are completely baked, I defy you to tell the difference. Such are the higher planes to-day of literary journalism, whence come the warnings to us sordid folk below, and the vulgar rich look up and turn away again (small blame to them) and build still larger soap-boxes on the green, and the "tired business-man" with averted eyes flees faster to the roof-garden, and Western colleges add new schools of dentistry with funds diverted from the "liberal arts"—and I am going to buy a paper collar and learn to chew tobacco if I can. Such "true refinement" would certainly be an appalling thing to have happen to one.

Why has no Anglo-Saxon writer taken the hint from M. Lemaitre's little paper on *le snobbisme littéraire* and carried the idea further? M. Lemaitre, of course, faltered miserably, for what could a Frenchman know of anything so intimately ours as *le snobbisme littéraire?* It is unfair to call it as some do an "academic" quality, thus debasing that honest word. Certainly detachment does not account for it, or a critical temper, or much reading,

173

or a contemplative habit. To write spiritlessly of spiritual things, to cheapen "what is most dear," to read merely to give advice, to make rules for genius and frame little definitions of greatness, to turn your back upon the crowd only that the crowd may see your back, to refer to vague standards and exhibit vague contempts—this is not the "academic" life. It is high life in Philistia, where the breath of one's nostrils is *le snobbisme littéraire.*

THE ART OF DISPARAGEMENT

VIII

THE ART OF DISPARAGEMENT

I HAVE lately read an inordinate amount of hostile criticism, especially as employed in literary controversy, drawn less by any expectation of learning the truth than by the hope of being warmed by the violent language. The point of view is the main point in hostile criticism, and yet it is the last point that the critic ever makes clear to the person whom he criticises. All my life long I have been sitting in judgment on other people and they on me. Had there been any means of executing the sentence, I should have hanged many of them, and I myself should have many times been hanged; but the arm of the law does not reach our pet aversions, and if it did, they would go to the gallows quite ignorant of the real nature of their offence. For criticism is very largely the art of assigning the wrong reason—a trumping up of sententious excuses, a straining after the point of view of society, or posterity, or the angels, or other critics, or the " cultivated few." Criticism stripped of its public robes of office is generally a private whim. That is what makes controversy often seem so strange to the non-combatants, especially literary controversy, turning as it does on private tastes which masquerade as public duties.

Here, for example, is our old friend, Professor Woodside, author of numerous volumes in praise of rusticity and the quiet life, and perhaps of a dozen others by the time this commentary appears, one of the most harmless of present writers. He paused for a moment some time ago and addressed a reply to his critics. They had taken, it seems, a moral tone with him, complaining that his insistence on the quiet virtues and contemplative life tended to unmanly acquiescence. Retorting in the same moral strain, he said there was no tendency in his writings to underrate the energies of active life but only to deny that the selfish desire of personal success was the proper motive for them. So it came to the usual *impasse* between a man and his critics. I hasten to assure any one whose hesitating eye may have travelled to this point that I am not going to discuss the moral tendency of Professor Woodside's books. I mention the matter merely as an instance of the hypocrisy of critics generally.

We belong to a race that dearly loves to moralise an essentially unmoral situation. We hide personal dislike behind moral disapproval if we can, and if there is any way of converting a private distaste into terms of public disaster, we find it. It is, I presume, bred in the bone, and I dare say, as a critic, I too should, if anybody poked me through the bars or set before me the food I did not like, utter the same irrelevant moral outcries, but that does not make the thing seem, in an honest interval, any less preposterous. It is too obvious that we damn people the deepest for the things they cannot help and love them for the random gifts of nature. We freely forgive all the rascals in literature from Benvenuto Cellini down —Sterne for his snivelling, Boswell for his truckling, Samuel Pepys for his mean little heart. We spend our days in invidiously rating one man above another and one woman above all others, edging away from estimable gentlemen at our clubs, dining with traitors. The rule applies as often in literature as in daily life that we could better spare a better

180

man. We all know it and we all act upon it, but I doubt if there has ever been an Anglo-Saxon critic who has not at some time lied about it.

The hypocrisy, of course, is in inverse ratio to the power of self-analysis. There are times when I half believe I hate Smith on principle, for there is nothing about Smith to lure me away from the most minute solicitude for the general good. In Smith's presence, the mind, having, as you may say, no personal interests, becomes intensely public-spirited and feels like a picket of the public conscience as against Smith, ready to shoot for hearth and country the moment a moral twig snaps. If the devil talked like Smith, what a pleasure to be a Christian soldier! In a sanguine mood I can almost prove that the devil does talk like Smith. Then along comes Jones, thrice as pernicious, but more beguiling, and not

one blow do I strike for an endangered uni-
verse, although Jones, reduced to a moral syl-
labus, Jones, issued in pamphlet form perhaps by one of Professor Woodside's critics,
would surely be an improper text-book for
the human race. But I would not have him
thus reduced. It is only when a living man
is no more to us than a teaspoon that we
think exclusively of his moral medicine to an
ailing world; and so it is with a living book.
Having no interest in Shakespeare as a poet,
Tolstoi and Mr. Bernard Shaw very naturally
hold him to strict account as a philanthro-
pist, missionary, Fabian lecturer, early Christian. When we are not amused, we remember
our moral lessons to humanity, and we can always find some large ennobling reason for not
being amused. If we do not love Shakespeare
let us say it is because Shakespeare did not
love the poor. And when it comes to the

"objective" critics, as they call themselves,
dissectors, classifiers, teachers of taste,
strange beings fatally absorbed in such problems as how to find the greatest common fac-
tor of Mark Twain and the Book of Job,
there is, I believe, little liking for any man's
company. That is why they so often cut out
the "central thought" of an author and
throw the rest of him away.

But to return to the subject of verbal con-
flicts, of which I have often been an inter-
ested observer. I once attended an important
encounter between Pragmatists and Anti-
pragmatists. A great many other ill-quali-
fied persons have had their say about Pragmatism, so why not I? To be sure, I cannot
settle offhand the question, What is Truth?
—at least not so completely but that a doubt
may linger in some minds after I have spoken.
But though I shall not insist on my authority

as a metaphysician, I do set up as a connoisseur of word-battles, with rather a pretty taste, never having missed, so far as I recall, any chance to overhear a literary altercation. Speaking, therefore, as an amateur of these savage spectacles, as a student of bitterness and rancour, of the lie given and returned, of the evasion, the cross-purpose, the word-trap, the moral bomb-shell, and the harsh laugh of logical supremacy, I do not hesitate to class the pragmatist polemics, in all that pertains to the noble art of wrangling, among the very best of recent misunderstandings. It is not too technical. Of course, if the anti-pragmatist really set out to find what the pragmatist was about, it might be difficult for us to follow, but philosophers fight like other men, and combat is not interpretation. They had rather thump a pragmatist than explain him, and quite right, too, and most fortunate for us outsiders, for a thump is clearer than an explanation. That is why we simple folk may, without impropriety, attend these pragmatistic encounters, for controversies are never philosophic even when philosophy is the theme; and when once the philosopher loses his head there remains nothing about him that need abash a common person.

The anti-pragmatists won two remarkable verbal triumphs. The first occurred in the following passage in a somewhat elaborate and altogether serious attack on Pragmatism:

"And now, to make matters perfectly clear, let us apply to this radical pragmatic meaning of truth the same illustration which was used in the preceding lecture to bring out the exact meaning of the correspondence theory. Poor Peter, you will remember, has a toothache, and John, who is thinking about his friend, has an idea that Peter has a toothache. As for the pragmatist the truth of an idea means its 'efficient working,' its 'satisfactoriness,' 'the process of verification,' the truth of John's idea will 'consist in' its satisfactoriness to John, in its efficient working, in its verifying itself. If it works, if it harmonises with John's later experiences of Peter's actions, if it leads in a direction that is worth while, it is true (a statement to which, indeed, all might assent), and its truth consists in this working, this harmony, this verification process. John's thought, the pragmatist insists, *becomes* true only when it has worked out successfully, only when his later experience confirms it by being consistent with it—for remember truth is not verifiability, but the process of verification. 'Truth happens to an idea. *It becomes* true, is *made* true by events.' At the time when John had the thought about Peter the thought was *neither true nor false,* for the process of verification had not yet begun, nothing had as yet happened to the idea. *It becomes* true, is *made* true by events, as John thought, but, all the same, John's thought was not true. It did not become true until several hours afterward—in fact, we may suppose, not until Peter, having cured his toothache, told John about it. The thought, ' Peter has a toothache,' thus as it happens, turns out not to have been true while Peter actually had the toothache, and to have become true only after he had ceased to have a toothache."

CONSTRAINED ATTITUDES

In like manner, another writer made short work of a certain essay on the Ambiguity of Truth—

The reader who will, throughout this essay on the ambiguity of truth, substitute "butter" for "truth" and "margarine" for "falsehood," will find that the point involved is one which has no special relevance to the nature of truth. There is "butter as claim," i. e., whatever the grocer calls butter; this, we will suppose, includes margarine. There is "butter validated," which is butter that, after the usual tests, has been found not to be margarine. But there is no ambiguity in the word "butter." When the grocer, pointing to the margarine, says, "This is butter," he means by "butter" precisely what the customer means when he says, "This is not butter." To argue from the grocer's language that "butter" has two meanings, one of which includes margarine, while the other does not, would be obviously absurd. Similarly when the rash man, without applying any tests, affirms "this belief is true," while the prudent man, after applying suitable tests, judges "this belief is not true," the two men mean the same thing by the word "true," only one of them applies it wrongly.

CONSTRAINED ATTITUDES

The spirit of these remarks is plain to the least technical of observers. It is not philosophy; it is war. No man in philosophic mood would ever have contrived that toothache pitfall; he would have doubted rather his own understanding. He would have consulted with pragmatists in advance—it was clearly a matter for consultation—and told them what a turn they had given him, how they seemed to say that if Peter had a toothache and John said so, John lied, but, of course, they could not mean it, and would they kindly explain what they did mean? And so of the other man—he would have gone straight to the enemy with his butter question, more in curiosity than in hatred, and asked for a plain statement of the pragmatist view of the butter-margarine relation, which is, I believe, Butter is as butter does. By going to him with his dilemma he could easily have had both horns of it removed, but he did not wish to do so. He wished to retain them for purposes of impalement. There you have the spirit of the conflict. When the battle mood is on him, one does not wish to understand the foeman. Time spent in understanding is time lost in battle, and no good word-fighter will ever seek an enemy's meaning when there are verbal shifts by which that enemy may be proved insane.

But in purely literary or journalistic fields of contest there is, I fear, not only a falling off in the quality of the indignation, but a growing reluctance on the part of journalists and men of letters to say the first hot, natural, senseless thing that occurs to them, thus diminishing what was once a source of lively public entertainment. Prizing as I believe most readers do any form of literary animation even when arising from bad blood, I always hasten to these scenes of verbal conflict in the hope of seeing manly blows exchanged. The eyes of the cat are greener and her tail is handsomer when she fights. It is not unreasonable to expect as much of authors. Self-love has ever been a rich literary vein. Admirable consequences have flowed from its wounds and many a good poem has followed a puncture. Great happiness has often been shed upon the world by the simple process of pricking an author. But in no recent literary encounter have I found anything at all commensurate with the hostile intentions—not a "Parthian dart," or an "envenomed shaft," or a "flick on the raw" or a "well-directed thrust," or any of the mordancies, causticities, pilloryings, unmaskings, witherings, and excoriations which connoisseurs in literary bitterness delight to describe. It has been a sad display of verbal impotence, humiliating to

190

two warlike Anglo-Saxon nations. Often the rage is barely articulate, passing off in mere brief cries of "fool," "clown," "driveller," and "mountebank," as if the hater had run short of breath. Somebody calls the enemy a "charlatan." Another says "self-advertiser" and lets it go at that,—a term, by the way, that applies as truly to the prophet as to the fool.

"Why do you box my ears in public?" said a well-known writer of the present day to his foeman, who had accused him of using too many words. Rather a sickly attenuation of the good, old-fashioned "reply to my critics." You have a "pygmy soul," wrote another warrior, and if Emerson were now living and should see you, Emerson would be "very much surprised." A playwright disliking a review of his play in a magazine, wrote to the editor, saying that the critic who wrote it was evidently quite "drunk," to which the editor replied that this was an "outrageous suggestion," for, as a matter of fact, he had written the article himself; and he went on to "confess" further "surprise" that "a man of your intellectual attainments should," etc., etc. Surprise, indeed, is a frequent weapon in these gingerly contests. Attack the average writer and he either retorts with an expression of "surprise" or remarks superbly that considering the character of his assailant he is "not at all surprised." His adversary then expresses amazement at this surprise. Why is surprise or the absence of it so highly esteemed for polemical purposes? Time and again I have been drawn by the promise of a good bout between literary egotisms, heard the hiss of the flying insult and the cry of the wounded vanity, seen the lie passing back and forth, and self-love stripped for action, only to find the whole thing going off in a mere popping of astonishments. "You're a Bayswater pessimist," was the angry editor's parting shot on this occasion. "You're a blazing boy," said the playwright fiercely. And each withdrew claiming the victory.

These are fair specimens of modern literary warfare. No spirit in either attack or defence; a nose-to-thumb gesture, a flounce, a swish of skirts, the banging of a distant door, both crow languidly, and so the battle ends without pleasure to the looker-on, pain to the victim, or relief to the assailant's feelings.

Shades of a thousand literary battlefields, how pitifully we have dwindled! There is not a good round curse amongst us, not a dangerous noun or prickly adjective. Tease an editor and out comes his pocket-handkerchief. He regrets and deplores the conduct of his adversary. He is very much surprised. It is, of course, most disappointing to the reader, who ought always to be *tertium gaudens* at these affairs.

Not that I would bring back the days of *The Dunciad* or of *English Bards and Scotch Reviewers.* You cannot ask an angry modern author to plan these long campaigns, or to rout the household out at midnight as Pope did in his transports of inspired malignity. But as a lover of the manly art (for others) I do object to this cheating of our gladiatorial expectations by exhibitions in spilt milk. For a literary fight is, after all, a public occasion. It is a promise of warmth and of heightened colour and we are justified in demanding some little excitement as we hasten to the field. It is unseemly that literary wrath, to which we are invited, should bring forth no fruit meet for publication.

Moreover, every honest writer is entitled to

at least one dangerous foe, none of your splutterers of "fool," "mountebank," and "mud prophets," but of the sort who will take pains in order to inflict them—whose rule for the arena shall be *Ita feri ut se sentiat mori,* or if that high standard cannot be attained, who will at least so strike that he will amuse the amphitheatre. And surely if a writer cannot fight well on so good an argument as his own self-love (often the most literary part of him), there will soon be an end to all sport for us spectators.

Nowadays when a critic is angry, he merely seems out of sorts, the wits being lost along with the temper. So the sting is drawn from the opposition, which is as bad for books as it is for politics. It does not mean an era of good feeling. It means an era of no feeling at all.

But here I seem to have fallen into the common error of rating the value of ridicule according to the pains of the intended victim. There is of course a risk in those customary comparisons between satire and teeth, stilettos, clubs, vitriol, bullets, scorpions, scalpels, gunpowder and harpoons. Though in good usage and of great antiquity, they are apt to raise our hopes too high. The scalds and perforations can seldom be authenticated, and even when they can, it does not follow that the ridicule is good. To read certain newspaper satires over again would be as deadly as anything they did to the victim. No man would do it, even were it proved that a maddened Chief Magistrate had fled to the jungle on account of them. I suppose I should not really value certain lines indited to a "woman with a serpent's tongue," even had the lady died of them. It is a mistake to measure literary merit by the damage it did at the time.

Literary people, accustomed as they are to

196

open their eyes very wide at one another and exalt the deeds of daring of the pen, have no idea what moderate creatures we readers really are. The most we can say of " envenomed shafts," as we know them nowadays, is that they sometimes almost tickle. The " merciless wit " of a leading article may at times compete with a breakfast muffin. Few sensations are less noticeable than these literary emotions that we ought to feel.

Even when speaking of good satire, writers often betray much confusion of mind. One of them has praised Pope's satire on Addison because it was so true that Addison must have felt ashamed. At this late day what do we care for Addison's guilty blushes? As lies about Addison they would serve our turn as well, for if Addison did not give his little Senate laws and sit attentive to his own applause, we know the man to do it—we might do it ourseives at a pinch. Permanent satire is not valued for the author's application but for private applications of our own. The best of satirists have never bagged their game. Nor is it necessary that a single reader shall be blasted; it is enough for him to hope that some one else is. All of which is obvious; yet we still go on reckoning the powers of ridicule in terms of estimated fool-destruction.

Now and then some one bitterly reminds us that what this country needs is a genuine satirist, which of course is true, but he goes on to depict a scene of quite incredible excitement— every fool up a tree, solemn folk exploding, self-complacency punctured, vice pilloried, humbug stripped, and a small number of very intelligent persons (himself among them) beside themselves for joy at the well-directed cuts, bites, burns, stings, and rapier-thrusts. Yet he knows as well as we do that we should

198

all come off without a scratch. When a great satire bursts upon the world the surprising thing has always been its utter harmlessness. The vices do not "slink to cover," the fool does not know he is being killed, the wounds of vanity all heal by first intention, and the deflated pomposities of our middle age fill again as naturally as the lungs do. And, after all, true satire is not the sneering substance that we know, but satire that includes the satirist. That is the grave omission of the usual satirist, the omission of himself—nearly all the world to the literary person yet left out of the world in almost every extremely sarcastic survey of it. There can of course be no sound derision of things *sub specie eternitatis* that does not include the blushing author. True satire is always self-ironical, and would have the whole world by the ears. While waiting for that very improbable man of genius to blow

199

up to the sky our follies and his own, we might
be doing useful work at the reduction of literary terms to a size more appropriate to the
little thoughts behind them.   But true satire
was not the aim of the verbal hostilities which I
have attended so eagerly these many years.
They sprang from grudges personal and bitter.   Their blows were aimed at single heads.
The tumult and the shouting promised well.
And though it was unreasonable to hope that
either warrior would be wounded fatally, they
might at least have been more accurately in-
sulting and more expressively enraged.

INTERNATIONAL IMPRESSIONISM

IX

INTERNATIONAL IMPRESSIONISM

WE no longer anthropomorphise the deity —at least not openly. The man who called his sermon " a bird's-eye view of God " is clearly an exception. Nor do we invoke in neat pentameters the personified emotions, tastes, branches of learning, scientific discoveries, trades and muses. No more of " All hail, oh Agriculture " or "Inoculation, heavenly maid, appear." But we make up for it with our philosophic wolves and thoughtful rabbits and melodramatic hens—no mere figures of rhetoric and beast fable, either, but certified of eye-witnesses, with affidavits, mind you, that cock-robin *was* killed by the sparrow with his little arrow. And especially there is the huge imagery of nations, so glib and definite, Germany in a word, Italy in a nut-shell, immoral France, stolid Britain, types, tendencies and signs of the times, all dancing around on the care-free pages of men whose sole aim is to make the best possible story out of the least possible experience, but who are ranged alongside De Tocqueville and other serious observers, as if that sort of thing were their aim. We still forget that they come not to see but to invent us.

We forget that for literary purposes this is not a country on the map. America is a happy guessing-ground, bounded on all sides by the Personal Equation and including many parallels of literary latitude. Its climate varies with the health of the visitor and its people have only such characteristics as a rapid writer can most effectively describe. It is, on the whole, entertainingly inhabited, with readable race traits, and concise, often epigrammatic, national ideals. Differences among the people are, as a rule, uninteresting and non-essential. The things that occur first to the literary visitor are at once the most significant and the best to say. The main products are unverifiable conclusions, which meet the traveller on every side; and, indeed, in sheer point of size are more impressive than the skyscrapers. The institutions, though varying with the mind's eye, are alike in yielding an immediate moral lesson. Everywhere you see the national pastime—matching with destiny for beers; everywhere the national tendency—declining like the Roman Empire, though perhaps that fate may be averted by the moral soundness which is at the bottom of the American character, as shown by two typical gentlemen in the smoking-room and three significant magazines.

CONSTRAINED ATTITUDES

Growth is wonderful, including the growth of the writer's convictions. The distances seem incredible. It is six hours from New York to Washington, and Chicago is even further from the truth; and there is room in the single State of Pennsylvania for several European generalities.

I have been moved to these remarks by reading the accumulated press clippings in regard to a most entertaining volume, which obviously belongs to this journalism of inverted pyramids, but was taken by Americans quite generally as an attempt to describe an actual country. They found the account " favourable." Had it been unfavourable they would no doubt have hurled back the insult in the author's teeth. The country is still gallantly defended in the newspapers against any scurrying foreigner's literary note-book. Apparently things have not changed much

since a boy of twenty-three brought down
upon his American notes the vengeance of
our staunch old home guard in the press
or since these same sleepless tutelary gentlemen repelled a redoubtable humorist or
argued gravely with the hereditary proclivities
of a French novelist and a German university
professor. Meanwhile most of us continue to
read these books for the pleasure they afford,
knowing that such truth as they contain is there
by accident. Who cares, for example, whether
the man is right or wrong? That is not the
kind of question to ask that kind of man. We
like these people for their impulsive ways and
general air of wildness. We want the fine swing
of certainty and plenty of prejudice and some
brisk invective and sarcasm and the first
thoughts after the first cocktail and the damnation of Chicago and a guess at the Middle
West and lots of large advice about abolishing

CONSTRAINED ATTITUDES

Congress and suppressing the rich and inter-
marrying with coloured people (as a solution of
the negro problem), and all that. We want the
writer's own particular America, the prolonga-
tion of his own blessed British, Gallic, Teu-
tonic, Slavic, bilious or sanguine, literary temperament, a land of personal patches with vast
areas of omission, peopled mainly by himself
and quivering with his emotions. To the well-
trained literary mind, phrase-haunted, fiction-
rooted, burning for the picturesque and sali-
ent, what is a country but a good excuse? Any
new land is a fairyland, and things are as they
look best in print. To bother him or our own
heads with vain questions of verisimilitude is,
to say the least, unsportsmanlike.

In this instance, the gigantesque journalist
admitted frankly that he had been in America
just six weeks, yet from one end of the country
to the other, to judge from these newspaper

comments, readers were asking if he was fair
and accurate and properly equipped for his
task. Many of them praised his " philosophic
insight," though how they knew he had it is
by no means clear. Some condemned him as
" superficial," as if any human being in the
circumstances could be otherwise; and some
complained that he was " inconclusive "—fancy
having to be conclusive about America in six
weeks. It must have embarrassed the modest
author, who had not in the least the air of a
Daniel come to the nation's judgment but of a
writer in search of literary incentives. As
well apply astronomical tests to verses to the
moon. We are still given over to great literal-
ness in these matters and cannot permit any
harmless light literary character to record his
ferry-boat emotions without harassing ourselves about the truth.

Of course, he and all the other recent

nation-tasters may, for aught I know, be profoundly and enormously right. The man who stoutly tells me what the matter is with Asia to-day, how Europe is feeling, and whether America ever can be cured always has me under his thumb. Not being stationed on a sign of the Zodiac I am in no position to reply. And why should one wish to deny by logic, comparative statistics, ethnology, political science, or indeed drag the intellect into the thing at all? Is it not pleasant to sit humbly by and see the populations of the earth " sized up," and hear Europe talking to America as man to man and learn the crisp truth about the Tropic of Capricorn, or the century, or modern society, or man? Need we be forever asking how he got his certitudes, and if it was the real America that met him in his boarding-house and if he surely grasped the negro problem while talking to those two coloured men?

CONSTRAINED ATTITUDES

Literary travel is not in search of fact but of fluency, and the route always lies away from the land of many things to the land where one swallow makes a summer.

Travel refreshes the faith in types. It is the rule of present-day *belles-lettres* that every country shall be peopled with types. At home men will not stay long in types, splitting up on acquaintance into mere personal and miscellaneous Browns and Robinsons, of small use for the larger literary purposes and refusing absolutely to typify mankind. As to Woman in General, that great literary science is often rudely shattered by sheer knowledge of one's wife. So off for a new land where everybody is an allegory. It may be safe for philosophers to stay and scrutinise, but for these brave, vivacious international certainties the land must be skimmed and the people merely squinted at; or they,

211

too, will resolve into Browns and Robinsons to the spoiling of good phrases and the blurring of bird's-eye views. The typical American is seen at once or never. There is no hope for any gigantesque journalist who does not find him on the pier. It is to get rid of facts, not find them, that they come, and to escape from second thoughts, those sad disturbers of literary traffic. It is not to see a new kind of man but to see the same kind newly.

But here is matter for peace-promoting societies and leagues of Anglo-American goodwill, for ambassadorial after-dinner speeches and toasts to distinguished guests, for almost simultaneously two books have appeared, one by an American who admires England and the other by an Englishman who admires America. As an American I suppose I ought to dwell long and earnestly on the cheerful import of this circumstance. For the American thinks it his duty to write on this subject as if he were fifty years behind his own feelings and the feelings of his fellow-countrymen. He assumes that the all-important question is whether the Englishman, no matter what sort of Englishman, thinks well or ill of the country as a whole. He assumes that this blushing little débutante of a country is still intensely anxious about the impression that it has made. It would astonish us if we were not so used to the strange archaisms of our daily press. But just as many newspaper writers are still at the Manchester stage of political economy, so their patriotism is of the tender period when Dickens published his *American Notes*. Journalists have always been our most old-fashioned class, being too busy with the news of the day to lay aside the mental habits of fifty years before. Constrained to chase the aviator in his aëroplane on the front page, they sleep with Thomas

CONSTRAINED ATTITUDES

Jefferson in the editorial columns. For a glimpse of the country's intellectual past we are accustomed to turn to the reflective portions of the morning newspapers. Reviewers live in the old tradition of patriotic solicitude while we have gone on into utter recklessness. I never met a man, for example, who seemed to care whether these visitors thought well or ill of the United States. I never read a review that did not.

In the friendly book about America the writer declares that he found among "all classes of Americans . . . a deep and noble desire . . . sometimes pathetic but always dignified" that the Mother Country should understand "her offspring of the West."

This is a very sentimental reading of the American's interest in the foreigner's opinion —a mere product of curiosity, self-consciousness and the desire to "make talk." If the writer, who, to judge from his book, is an uncommonly serious person, found everybody nobly and deeply concerned with the Mother Country's opinion, it was no doubt the result of conversational embarrassment. With a serious Briton on one's hands, what else was there to do? Those of us who have had conversational bouts with serious Britons recall the desperate straits to which we were often reduced, the false interests, the impromptu enthusiasms, the nervous garrulities, merely to keep the ball rolling. One finds one's self becoming almost hysterically sociable with phlegmatic persons. If one man says too little, the other says too much. It seems a law of conversation that if one remain a centre of gravity the other shall with rather foolish rapidity revolve around him. He feels responsible for the other's lack of animation—

tries to bring a gleam into the cold, dead eye.
An American is unnerved by the British pause
following an introduction. He will snatch at
any topic and cling to it out of sheer mental
loneliness. He is not accountable at these
times, and the meaning of what he says will
not bear scrutiny. No American is ever himself in the spurt of talk following those tense
moments when, a serious Briton having been
cast upon him, the beating of his own heart
was the only sound he heard. He will profess
the most unnatural ardours—asking after a
stranger's country as he asks after a friend's
wife: not because he finds the wife interesting,
but because he hopes she interests the friend.
People spoke warmly of the Mother Country
in order to warm this visitor. We overheat
our conversation as we do our rooms.

The American writer on England, on the
other hand, had not even this excuse for his
delicacy and forbearance. No polite disguise

covers the stark indifference of the English to American opinion, and he himself remarks how invulnerable their feelings are.

Yet after a long black list of national hypocrisies, he says:

"I write these things to explain, not to revile. This is a great country."

And referring to the newspaper practice of selecting only the worst news of rival countries —crimes, disasters, scandals, he says he forbears to impute any unworthy motive.

Such assumptions of judicial moderation are of course quite thrown away. In the familiar field of international impressionism we do not look for the "clear, white light of truth," but for the colours of personal experience. The chief value of these books consists, as I have said before, in their re-discovery of human nature.

Thus the American impressionist's book contains an entertaining chapter on England as the "land of compromise," arraying antithetically the pretended virtues and the actual vices, the criticism of others and the self-complacency, and presenting a most formidable list of inconsistencies, thus:

A King who is not a King; a free people who are not actually free; a constitution which does not exist; a nation professing Christianity, but always at war, sodden with drink, and bestowing the highest prizes on the selfish and the strong; high principles sacrificed to expediency; personal freedom politically fettered by a House of Lords; contempt for commercial rivals and blindness to the danger of their competition; an inveterate preference for doing rather than thinking. And in the face of the various "new problems "—"disestablishment," "unemployment," "increased taxes," "socialism," foreign rivalry and hatreds—no new weapon has been found!

All of which is accidentally British, but essentially of course it is only human—mere marks of the *zoön politikon*. Under the same rhetorical arrangement each land in turn becomes the land of compromise. They are home truths, but without the local colour. This is saying nothing against it as a chapter in international impressionism. On the contrary, comparative reflections would have impaired the vivacity. The best way to find new types is to forget the old. After all, dilettantes in the psychology of races do not compete with the hard-headed grubbing specialists. Sizing up a nation in this way is just as interesting as ever. The literary man is a born multiplier. It is easy for him to characterise a country; his imagination has peopled it. Observe the astonishing similarity between the Manchester bottle-maker whom Matthew Arnold found to be perfectly typical of England and the

Oneida chain-maker who " illuminated " for a recent British visitor "much that had hitherto been dark in the American character." " His ignorance," says Matthew Arnold of this peculiarly British bottle person, "his ignorance of the situation, his ignorance of what makes nations great, his ignorance of what makes life worth living, his ignorance of everything except bottles—those infernal bottles." " Making a new world," says the British observer of this utterly American maker of chains, " was, he thought, a rhetorical flourish about futile and troublesome activities, and politicians merely a disreputable sort of parasite upon honourable people who made chains and plated spoons." International impressionists traverse the world to discover the people who live next door. So we owe this lively chapter about England as the land of compromise, not to the writer's perception of what is characteristically British, but to his revived interest in original sin.

This particular international impressionist found England a land of success-worship where all's well that sells well, and the weakest go to the wall, where the problem of serving both God and Mammon has been solved; and as his heart is on the side of the big battalions, he loves her all the better on that account. He accepts all ideas at their present commercial rating. Success can do no wrong and the best man comes to the top, and what will become of England's greatness if she pampers her poor? Beware of discouraging thrift. The virtues pay and thus we may know they are virtues; and away with socialistic nostrums. In books so casually compounded it is absurd to look for a pattern in the rags and patches of their thoughts. Thought, after all, this wise Polonius might say, is a branch of etiquette; give us the deeds without the thoughts; find out what souls are worn in the better sort of houses and order one of the same for yourself. It will keep you with the best Society of your day as in lustier times it would have kept you a cannibal. If I had to define this appraiser of nations I should perhaps say that in religion he was a good digestionist, in politics a Darwinian and in philosophy, while I am not learned enough to place him, I know he belonged somewhere in an anti-pragmatist definition of their enemies. But having a light heart and a half-closed mind and a frank pride in his limitations he was just the man for international impressionism, and gave us as good a bit of it as we had had for several years. I suppose he must rank rather high among the nation-tasters.

In this pleasant but unconscionable pastime there is nothing so untidy as exceptions, and nothing will more surely spoil a sentence than thinking twice. It checks the flow of firm conviction if after every telling paragraph you write, "On second thoughts this is not true." Nor is it by any means needful. Readers of international impressionism ought by this time to have the converse of almost every proposition ringing in their ears as they read.

QUOTATION AND ALLUSION

X

QUOTATION AND ALLUSION

THE old tradition lingers that quotations or bookish allusions will give the look of literature to any printed page. Sometimes it is followed on the chance that scraps from the works of better writers may somehow tide the reader over when the man's own thoughts give out—a clutch at the skirts of literary gentility in the hope of redeeming a natural insignificance. Sometimes it is to show that he is a man of varied reading, each quotation serving as an apothecary's diploma that none may deny that he has graduated from the book. At all events, it usually has the air of deliberation, as if the quotation had not come to the man, but the man had gone to the quotation.

CONSTRAINED ATTITUDES

In the old days there were of course some involuntary quoters, to wit, Burton, in the *Anatomy*, who could not help bubbling over with queer, outlandish sayings that he had picked up just for fun. But the typical quoter was a university man, who, before he wrote a paragraph, went on a pot-hunt among the Latin poets in order that he might cite triumphantly twenty-four lines of Virgilian metaphor beginning, " Not otherwise a Nubian lion with his tawny mane." He often fastened them to the context by invisible threads, merely saying, " As the ancient bard hath so well remarked," and pulling out a block of Latin hexameters from a drawer in his desk. He could not speak of agriculture without dragging in the Georgics, or of old age without a phrase from Cicero, or of love or wine without a couplet from Horace. He simply had to use these things, to say nothing of Prætorian guards,

Pierian spring, Parnassus, Arethusa and those poor old raddled muses.

He and his kind multiplied like Australian rabbits, and it was not till the middle of the last century that English literature began to drive them out. Nowadays we are comparatively safe from them, and no one with any natural spring of mind ekes out his thought with other people's phrases. The rule to-day is neither to shun nor to seek.

In these days, if a man have a little Latin or Greek, the good safe working rule is to keep it strictly to himself, when his native idiom will serve as well, though he is likely to burst with his happy secret. We stow these collegiate scraps away in the back part of our dictionaries. Everyone knows where to find them, and nobody thanks the man who takes them out. The writers of a hundred or even fifty years ago are no guides for us in this matter.

CONSTRAINED ATTITUDES

When Burke wrongly accented a Latin word all Parliament knew it, and Wyndham was vastly admired for the enormous length of his Latin quotations. Now the whole point of the thing is gone. Were the best of the old writers living now they would never have the air of being " echo-haunted of many tongues." Of that we may be certain. Even Thackeray would be more sparing of his *pallida mors*, and would sometimes omit the Latin form of his " black care behind the horseman."

But although we have in the main discarded inapplicable Latin and Greek, here and there the old precedent of needless quotation is still followed, and only the other day I read in a newspaper article, " If a thing is right, it ought to be done, said Cobden," recalling the old gibe that water is wet on the authority of Beza. I have noted the same bit from a foreign language nine times in one newspaper, and each time could see the paragraph writhing to make room for it. The Vicar of Wakefield's friend, with his two stock phrases from the classics, seems almost a burlesque, but he was not, and he is not even to-day. There are men now living who will use a French word when there is an exact English equivalent, and then add the equivalent in parentheses—a vile form of ostentation and half-hearted at that, a sentence like a moustache with one end waxed and the other bushy, as if the writer dared to be only half-way foppish. There are wretches who will quote you Pascal for the sentiment that truth will prevail. "Corrupt politics are not good politics," says Burke, and "Life is a struggle," says Seneca, and "Dare to do right," says Cobden, and "Law is the bulwark of liberty," as the Lord Chief Justice of England once remarked. The hardened quoter cares only for the name, and perhaps, when pressed for time, will forge it. That may be why one sees so many dull sayings with great names attached. But many, of course, are genuine, and toilsomely gathered for use on the day of literary deficit, when the style needs a ringlet from Longfellow, or an orotund boom from Burke.

I find, for example, in a recent number of the *Didactic Monthly*, a writer of extraordinary literosity. In a scant two pages I note quotations from Disraeli, John Morley, Thiers, Condorcet, Garfield, Seneca, Tacitus, Milton, Lincoln, Thucydides, President Harrison, Cobden, and Disraeli again; also several illustrative literary anecdotes, one Latin verse, and three lines of a poem in English. He ought not to have done it. It makes us ignorant persons envious. Even when we do know, we must sometimes try and forget, for it is cruel to be as " literary " as you can. Not that I deny the appositeness of all these literary allusions, but a good many of them served only to show in what company the writer had been. They were, as you might say, merely his literary credentials, and even as such are less convincing than in the brave old days when there were no Dictionaries of Quotation or treasuries of prose or verse or Half Hours with Great Authors or Libraries of the World's Best Literature. It is a humane rule never to jingle your literary pockets merely to tantalise the poor.

Had one a good literary memory or a full note-book (which can be made to look as well) one might retort upon these learned Thebans somewhat in this wise: New kings are strict, said Æschylus (*hapas de trachus hostis an neon krate*), and he might well have said it of the newly learned, for they too abate no jot of their authorities, but approach all subjects augustly, clad in the robes of their predecessors. And for crown jewels, they have those " jewels five words long," which they never weary of displaying. Nor do they forget that Milton's style was " echo-haunted of many tongues," the style for which he became so famous and so shunned. They stay very close to Milton. But they ignore, alas, many wise sayings even from the time of the Chaldees. There was Elihu's warning, " Should a wise man utter vain knowledge and fill his belly with the east wind? " And there was Quintilian, who, if I mistake not, implied that whoso would seem learned to the vulgar seemeth vulgar to the wise. Plato himself was against them, defending not the borrowing of treasures merely for display, but praising rather the mind's activity with its own possessions, and a certain high inspired curiosity, for, said he, " a life without inquiry (*anexetastos bios*) is not livable

CONSTRAINED ATTITUDES

by man." And from Plato we may pass to
John P. Robinson, of whom it is perhaps super-
fluous to quote the well-known lines:

> John P.
> Robinson, he
> Said they didn't know everything
> Down in Judee.

Nor is that reading the most fruitful which
yields the quickest crop, particularly if it be
only a crop of quotations, for that is like dig-
ging up your seed potatoes. A mind planted
with the world's best authors must still wait for
its own thoughts to grow, for, as Cicero said,
all the arts have a common element (*quoddam
commune vinculum*), and it is as true of letters
as of agriculture that, as Sir Thomas Brown
has somewhere tersely put it, "All celerity
should be contempered by cunctation." Scraps
from a great man's writings are no sign of a
sense of greatness, but many quote them as

235

clear proof that they have seen Behemoth and " played with him as with a bird." As Confucius said to Julius Cæsar, " Be to thine own self true," and this implies that you have a self, a poor thing, but thine own, submerged by other people's words, but still sentient, a pale survivor of ten thousand tags and hackneyisms like these which I have used. Something off your own bat (to use a coarse postclassic figure) is wanted now and then. One learns little more about a man from the feats of his literary memory than from the feats of his alimentary canal.

When young and helpless I once fell into a family that lived by the bad old rule. They made it a daily duty to study up things to quote, and every Sunday morning at breakfast each would recite a passage memorised during the week. The steam from the coffee vanished

into literary air, and the muffins, by the time
we got to them, seemed to be bound in calf.
They said it helped to fix the thing in mind,
and though they had no present use for it,
they thought something might happen that it
would seem to fit. And they saw to it that
something did happen, and out it came to the
end. They lived in a sort of vicious watchful-
ness. On wet days they conned over their rain
verse in order to whip out a stanza in the midst
of weather talk, and if they drove through the
country they saw nothing for constantly
mumbling what Wordsworth would have said.
They would say the passage was doubtless familiar, but relentlessly repeat every word.
Large blocks of poetry would suddenly fall
athwart the conversation, no one knew whence,
while with bowed head the startled Philistine
would wait for the seizure to pass. There was

nothing in that family that you could not somewhere read, and the people who once knew them, now either visit a library or turn to an album of song. To be sure it was somewhat unusual, but it shows there is life in the old temptation, and what havoc it still may work.

OCCASIONAL VERSE

XI

OCCASIONAL VERSE

THEY say the modern man does not read poetry. I have read many essays on the growing dislike for it, and I remember particularly one very sad interview with a London publisher which appeared in a British periodical under the appropriate caption, " The Slump in Verse." I recall, too, some lines in *Punch* written at that time, telling us that the case was hopeless—

`For men in these expansive times
    (Due, I am told, to fiscal freedom),
Though earth were black with angels' rhymes,
    Dine far too well to want to read 'em.

Yet looking back on the past decade I cannot escape the conviction that it has been one of extraordinary prosodical activity. Occasional verse has never been so abundant or so prompt, for poets nowadays are great readers of the newspapers, especially of the headlines, and trained to sing before the report is contradicted, almost between successive editions.

Now I, who never drank of Aganippe well, nor ever did in Vale of Tempe sit, may not speak with authority in these deep matters, but as a warm-hearted fellow-being, anxious to see every poet, great or small, put his best foot foremost, I may venture to remind them of the notoriously small proportion of occasional verse that has ever succeeded in rising to the occasion. This is the more needful because when a poet goes wrong he is forgotten, and so the warning is lost. The fugitive poet almost invariably makes his escape, which is not a wholesome example. I recall several poetical occasions of the last ten years, unjustly forgotten by everybody else, for they deserve remembrance for the damage that was done.

In the first place there was the South African war. It was not in South Africa alone that Englishmen were called upon to face the horrors of that war. The kind of verses that were cabled to us from England every few days appealed almost as strongly to our sympathies as the reports of casualties from the front. One after another the leading poets of England tried and failed. One group of them clinging to classic models, achieved only alliteration and Homeric metaphors. These were not content till they had employed the expression "Afric's shores." Others, mad after colloquialism, were impelled by their strictly democratic conscience to use the word "bloomin'" in every fourth line. Of the two, the "bloomin'" ballad was preferable because less pretentious, less like a deliberate assault upon the muse, and when it was a frank appeal for subscriptions to some charity, it may have been justified by the pecuniary results. It was bad enough, however, and the "Afric's shore" things were quite unpardonable. When England reckoned up her victories she had as offset several scores of punctured poets that never again could be quite what they once were to the public.

And in France there were Rostand's lines on poor old President Krüger. "No," sang the poet, "history has nothing in her cycles finer or more tragic than the spectacle of this old man in eyeglasses with crêpe on his hat"—a bald rendering of the French verse, I admit, but it deserves no better. Some one commented on it rather sadly at the time as proof of "a faltering pen and laboured inspiration," which, of course, was most unjust as applied to merely occasional verse. It was as good as most of it. Setting the news of the day to music is a hard task, and the best of poets need a piano-tuner if you insist on banging out an accompaniment on them to every press despatch. And besides there were some swift readers in that day who no doubt found much beauty in that line, *Avec ce crêpe à son chapeau!* He would have been asked to read it at an authors' meeting in this country, and friends might have crowded around and grasped his soft, moist hand, and told him it was the best thing he had ever done; and within two weeks he might have been lecturing on it before the Burial Society and squaring it with world politics at the Kansas Woman's Club.

For who are we that we should revile these efforts of the foreigner? To be sure during the war with Spain our bards were more forbearing and we were singularly free from martial poetry of this class. Yet we had poets who put up pumping stations at the Pierian Spring, poets who supplied the public dinner table, who, no matter what the public occasion, had as fixed a place at it as music by the band, stem-winding poets ever ready to "read some little thing," bards of a strange and passionate promptness, surprised may be, yet turning quickly on the tormentor and ripping out an ode. And of all the odes that ever burst punctually from a poet's heart on the mornings of anniversaries, odes on unveilings, flag-hoistings and layings of corner-stones, odes on first shovelfuls and final bricks, odes obituary, natal, royal-matrimonial, sesqui-centennial, and millenary, this country has undoubtedly produced odes the most perfectly occasional, odes the most utterly commemorative.

As soon as the report of the St. Petersburg massacre reached England and America, most of the small poets and one or two of the larger ones set vigorously to work, and in an almost incredibly short time the mails were full of poems on the Czar. It was not my fortune to see many of them, but from such as happened my way and from the reports of readers who occupied a more exposed position, I inferred that either the later ones were all modelled on the first or that by a marvellous coincidence forty independent inspirations hit on the self-same words. So embarrassing was the situation that one newspaper announced that it could not publish any more poetical rebukes of the Czar except on the impossible condition that they contained thoughts not presented in those already printed; and it decided in advance against any poem that should turn on the incongruity between the Czar's title of "Little Father" and his unpaternal conduct toward his people. It seemed that twenty poets a day were discovering that incongruity.

And since this has happened many times

247

these past ten years, if indeed something like it has not been constantly going on, it seems as if the thousand men and women now engaged on songs appropriate to the press despatches should somehow be reminded of the simple truth. For despite many conspicuous exceptions it is well known that even great poets have always done their worst when keeping these public engagements. Banquets, birthdays, coronations, bicentennials, news from the seat of war, the laying of corner-stones, earthquakes, assassinations, the return of heroes, the thousand and one obviously poetic exigencies of the day, have been sung in the lays that are hardest to remember. Poets are by nature unpunctual and perverse and of the least use when in the greatest hurry to make themselves useful. It has been proved that the best poems are those which we did not know were wanted and that the worst are those which are deliv-

ered on demand; and that occasional verse, being of the latter description, merely darkens a
little the day or the deed, or the lady's album
that called it forth. Where genius has so
often failed, it seems as if our milder, modern
bards might observe more prudence, and await
more patiently the birth of song, realising
that it is given to few poets to take time by
the forelock, or make hay while the sun shines,
or strike while the iron is hot—adages not
meant for bards but for farmers, steamfitters
and us old prosers, who are as inspired to-day
as we ever shall be and stand no chance of a
tuneful impulse if we wait for ever so long.